Presented To:

_____

From:

_____

Date:

_____

Glimpses of an Invisible God
for Mothers

HB
HONOR
BOOKS

07 06 05 04 03   10 9 8 7 6 5 4 3 2 1

Glimpses of an Invisible God for Mothers
ISBN 1-56292-880-5
Copyright © 2003 by Honor Books
An Imprint of Cook Communications Ministries
4050 Lee Vance View
Colorado Springs, Colorado 89018

Developed by Bordon Books

Manuscript written by Vicki Kuyper and Stephen Parolini in conjunction with Bordon Books.

Introduction

More than ever before, people are searching—longing for a deeper relationship with God. Most have no problem recognizing His distinguished hand in the bright hues of the rainbow, the magnificent grandeur of the night sky, the breathtaking vistas of the Grand Canyon. But many of these seekers hope for more. *Is God present in the routine moments of my everyday life?* they wonder.

If you have been asking that question, *Glimpses of an Invisible God for Mothers* was written just for you. As you move through its pages, you will visit the everyday existence of men, women, and mothers just like yourself, and you will have an opportunity to learn how they are experiencing God in both the great and small details of their lives.

We know you will be blessed as you discover the depth of God's love for you and His commitment to walk with you as you discover *Glimpses of an Invisible God* in your own life as a woman and as a mother.

"Have I not commanded you?
Be strong and of good courage;
be not frightened, neither be dismayed;
for the LORD your God is
with you wherever you go."

JOSHUA 1:9 RSV

In the day when I cried out, You answered me,
and made me bold with strength in my soul.
Though I walk in the midst of trouble,
You will revive me.

PSALM 138:3,7 NKJV

I can do everything with the help of Christ
who gives me the strength I need.

PHILIPPIANS 4:13 NLT

Get Back on Your Feet

Three-year-old Cole squirmed in his car seat with anticipation of his trip to the park. Cammie watched him from her rearview mirror. He clapped his hands, wiggled his feet and smiled at his mommy in the mirror. "Slide—slide—" Cole said.

He could hardly wait for his feet to reach the sidewalk as Cammie took him out of the car. He raced to the slide. "Cole," Cammie called, "wait for Mommy." She pulled the ice chest and blanket from the trunk of the car. "Cole, wait . . . "

It was too late. Cammie looked up just in time to see Cole plummeting to the bottom of the slide. Cammie dropped everything in her arms and rushed to Cole. "Son, I asked you to wait." Tears trickled down Cole's face as Cammie hugged him tightly. Then she stood him up and brushed him off.

"I slid-did," Cole smiled through his tears.

"Yes, and you can go back up and do it again," Cammie told him, this time waiting at the bottom of the slide. "Mommy's here to catch you, just in case." *Just like God waits to catch me when I get ahead of Him,* Cammie thought.

God is always there to help us back to our feet.

"I have loved you with an everlasting love."

JEREMIAH 31:3 NASB

Restore us, O God; make your face
shine upon us, that we may be saved.

PSALM 80:3

Like an open book, you watched me
grow from conception to birth;
all the stages of my life were spread out
before you, the days of my life all
prepared before I'd even lived one day.

PSALM 139:16 THE MESSAGE

A Good Idea

"**M**om, where would I be if I wasn't borndid?"

Karen groaned. At three, Andrew was a child philosopher if ever there were one. She could count on him to lay a mind-boggling question on her at every bedtime.

"Well, Andrew, you would be in God's mind just ready to come out because you are such a good idea He couldn't help but think you up."

Andrew's big brown eyes took this in. "I would think you, Mommy, if I was God. You are a good idea too."

Karen hugged Andrew and fought back the tears that welled up from somewhere deep inside.

"I would like to be a good idea, God," she whispered later as she waited for Nathan to come in from the late shift. The quiet of the house grew and surrounded her like a big, fuzzy blanket. Her heart yearned for God's approval.

As she sat in the the quiet, she felt God say to her. "You have it, child." She never forgot the tears of joy that flooded her face.

Sometimes the demands of your life can make you feel inadequate. Always remember you have God's love. You are His joy.

There is no surprise more magical than the surprise of being loved. It is the finger of God on a person's shoulder.

Make it your ambition to lead a quiet life.

1 THESSALONIANS 4:11

Let the peace of God rule in your hearts.

COLOSSIANS 3:15 KJV

"And in this place I will give peace,"
says the Lord All-Powerful.

HAGGAI 2:9 NCV

*The greater part of our happiness
depends on our disposition
and not our circumstances.*

The Din

Margaret reluctantly loaded the children into the car for yet another birthday party at one of those children's "theme" restaurants. The children giggled and chattered with anticipation, but their excitement only served to make Margaret dread the experience more. Children of all ages screaming, yelling, crying, and downing lots of forgettable pizza. Bells and buzzers sounding off in unpredictable rhythms. Music blaring from dozens of wall-mounted speakers. Lights flashing.

After the birthday formalities had been dispensed, Margaret asked a friend to watch her children for a few minutes, and she stepped outside to escape the din. Before she returned to the party, Margaret bowed her head and thanked God for her children and the privilege of seeing their faces light up with childish wonder and delight. It took only a glimpse of the gift of her children whom God had given her to put things in perspective.

Do you need to find time for God in the midst of your busy day?

Give me an undivided heart.

PSALM 86:11

Commit everything you do to the Lord.
Trust him to help you do it and he will.

PSALM 37:5 TLB

If you find life difficult because you're
doing what God said, take it in stride.
Trust him. He knows what he's doing,
and he'll keep on doing it.

1 PETER 4:19 THE MESSAGE

In Focus

Brianne was the queen of multitasking. She carpooled six children to school while talking on her cell phone. Prayer time was no exception. But when she talked to God He had her full attention. She had tried talking to Him at the gym or while doing the dishes, and something was missing when she did it.

She still talks to God while dishwashing and when she takes a walk, but the time she spends in her "prayer chair" in the quiet of the morning has become a very special time. God can talk to her because she has quieted herself to listen. Sometimes her plans for an entire day change because of what He tells her that morning. Sometimes when she lays out a schedule that overwhelms her and that she just can't face, God answers with strength or with a flurry of phone calls from people canceling meetings for the day.

Brianne feels loved because she sets aside time each day so God can care for her.

Give God your undivided attention, and you'll be able to experience His undivided attention to you!

God and man exist for each other, and neither is satisfied without the other.

I will praise the Lord, who counsels me;
even at night my heart instructs me.

PSALM 16:7

We also glory in tribulations,
knowing that tribulation produces
perseverance; and perseverance,
character; and character, hope.

ROMANS 5:3-4 NKJV

I am sure that God who began the
good work within you will keep right
on helping you grow in his grace until
his task within you is finally finished.

PHILIPPIANS 1:6 TLB

Unexpected Answers

"Somebody's got to keep the company afloat," John muttered as he fell asleep. Since John's boss had quit, late nights had become the norm. Each night Deborah watched John, exhausted, fall into a restless sleep. She often fell asleep praying for him, and this night was no different.

The next thing she knew, John was frantically bailing water out of a leaky rowboat, but the storm was winning. Deborah feared he was going to drown. She cried out to God for help. A deep peace settled over Deborah, and she awoke. It had been a dream, but the peace remained. God had been there even as she slept.

That day John came home and said many of the people who still had faith in the company's success had agreed to help him. John confessed, "I think it is time to accept the help of my coworkers. And, Honey, I need your help, too, or I'm sunk."

God has His own secret stairway into every heart.

"You have it, dear," she said, hugging him. And silently she thanked God for answering her prayers.

Do you pray for your husband and children? God will hear you if you do.

Let us draw near to God with a sincere heart.

HEBREWS 10:22

When a believing person prays,
great things happen.

JAMES 5:16 NCV

The Lord will answer when I call to him.

PSALM 4:3 NLT

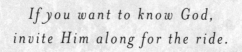

*If you want to know God,
invite Him along for the ride.*

A Drive in the Country

Marsha had been driving this route for nearly thirty years. Her aging mail truck seemed to steer on its own, so familiar was it with the gritty gravel roads and the rich country air. Leaving this job wasn't going to be easy. She'd miss the people: Miss May and the litters of new puppies each spring, Connie and her horribly burned but generously offered cookies.

But mostly she'd miss the drive. No, it wasn't that her truck seat was all that comfortable. Duct tape barely contained the springs straining to escape the vinyl. And it wasn't the quiet ride—though most of the creaking, sputtering, and coughing noises had become her old friends by now.

For thirty years, Marsha had spent every driving moment in prayer. She prayed for her customers, her family, and for a closer relationship with God. *I'm thankful for the peaceful times when I caught a glimpse of an invisible God during my day,* she thought.

What place does prayer have in your life?

I delight greatly in the Lord;
my soul rejoices in my God.

ISAIAH 61:10

We are ambassadors for Christ,
God making his appeal through us.
We beseech you on behalf of Christ,
be reconciled to God.

2 CORINTHIANS 5:20 RSV

Your awe-inspiring deeds
will be on every tongue;
I will proclaim your greatness.

PSALM 145:6 NLT

A Great Day

Somewhere around noon, Bekka's less-than-perfect day changed. That's when Dorothy called. "Aaron just called from the office, Bekka. He's not going to be laid off after all. But that's not the whole story. You aren't going to believe this—he's going to be heading up a new division! He got a promotion!"

Dorothy shared detail after detail about the dramatic turn-around in Aaron's office. The joy Bekka heard in her voice was a welcome change from the months of tears and turmoil.

"Bekka," continued Dorothy, "I know you've been praying for us and all . . . and . . . well, I don't know how that works . . . but maybe it . . . well . . . thanks. Maybe you could show me how to know God better." Bekka's heart was filled with indescribable warmth. What great news! *It's turning out to be a great day,* she thought.

Prayer is our greatest daily connection with God. Share it with someone today.

Our prayer and God's mercy are like two buckets in a well; while the one ascends, the other descends.

I'll make a list of God's gracious dealings,
all the things God has done
that need praising, all the
generous bounties of God.

ISAIAH 63:7 THE MESSAGE

Oh, give thanks to the Lord!
Call upon His name; make known
His deeds among the peoples!

1 CHRONICLES 16:8 NKJV

Thanks be to God, who always leads us
in the triumphal procession in Christ
and through us spreads everywhere the
fragrance of the knowledge of him.

2 CORINTHIANS 2:14

Legacy of Love

Finding the right wedding gift for her only child, Jennifer, wasn't going to be easy. After all, how do you say, "I love you," "I'm happy for you," "I'm going to miss you," and "I'll be praying for you" all at once? But then she caught sight of the frayed binding of a deep blue journal. She knew God had opened her eyes to the perfect gift.

Almost every morning since her own wedding day, Rebecca had written down God's answers to prayer in that journal. Recorded in it were her longings for a child, as well as her words of gratitude that God had given her Jennifer. The journal held a record of twenty-five years of God's faithfulness to her family. Now, it was time to pass on that legacy to her daughter to remind her of the kinds of miracles God would also do in her own life.

Are you recording the blessings God brings to your life? Perhaps it's time to begin.

God gave us memories that we might have roses in December.

My troubles turned out all
for the best—they forced me
to learn from your textbook.

PSALM 119:71 THE MESSAGE

In him all the treasures of wisdom
and knowledge are safely kept.

COLOSSIANS 2:3 NCV

This is what the Sovereign LORD says:
"I myself will search and find my sheep."

EZEKIEL 34:11 NLT

*The Bible is a letter from God
with our personal address on it.*

Three Weeks in Bed

"Three weeks in bed." That's what the doctor had said. For the hundredth time in the last two days, Tasha reached over to grab the television remote. Instead, she knocked it onto the floor. She heard the familiar sound of cracking plastic, followed by the unfamiliar, yet easy-to-identify sound of triple-A batteries rolling across the wooden floor. The kids were at school—no one could pick them up for her.

Tasha looked around her room at the shelves filled with trophies—soccer, cheerleading, and the dance trophies she and her husband had won. "Three weeks in bed." That's what the doctor had said. But then he'd continued: ". . . and a few months of rehabilitation. In time, we expect you'll be as good as new."

"Three weeks in bed." And now no remote. Tasha reached out to the bedside table and fumbled around, trying to find a book. She did—her Bible. As she lifted it up and started to open it, she felt God saying, "Finally, I have your undivided attention. I love you!"

Don't wait until you're flat on your back to discover the world's most important Person!

"Rejoice that your names
are written in heaven."

LUKE 10:20

The good man—what a different story!
For the good man—the blameless,
the upright, the man of peace—
he has a wonderful future ahead of him.
For him there is a happy ending.

PSALM 37:37 TLB

"Whoever believes in Him should not
perish but have eternal life."

JOHN 3:15 NKJV

It All Works Out in the End

Yolanda's world seemed like a playground full of bullies. Office bullies stole accolades and stymied promotions. Neighborhood bullies drove trucks across her lawn and complained about her oil-spewing car. And her ex-husband had been given joint custody of their daughter, Amanda, whom he had never called or visited until now.

Yet as she walked through her "playground," Yolanda wasn't afraid or bitter. Yes, her mother still tried to run her life. A coworker would probably take credit for another of her great ideas. And she still had to share joint custody of Amanda. But to Yolanda, these events were just part of life. Besides, she knew that a better place awaited her at the end of this sometimes unfair existence. One day there would be a heavenly playground that would offer nothing but fun.

Keep Heaven on your mind when you encounter injustice. That promise will provide a ray of light—a glimpse of God—whenever you are tempted to feel resentful.

The best part of God's good news is that it gets even better.

Devote yourselves to prayer,
being watchful and thankful.

COLOSSIANS 4:2

As you therefore have received Christ Jesus
the Lord, so walk in Him, rooted and
built up in Him and established in the faith,
as you have been taught,
abounding in it with thanksgiving.

COLOSSIANS 2:6-7 NKJV

Let your heart therefore be
wholly true to the Lord our God,
walking in his statutes and keeping
his commandments, as at this day.

1 KINGS 8:61 RSV

Uphill Climb

"Baby steps, baby steps . . ." Glenda reminded herself as she made her way up the face of the rocky cliff. It had taken her awhile to master rock-climbing techniques, with plenty of missteps along the way. Although climbing took her total focus, she couldn't get her mind off the argument she had just had with her son.

Sixteen-year-old Jason lacked focus—commitment to school, work, almost anything. He seemed angry and unresponsive. Glenda had seen some changes over the past few months, but they were small and infrequent. At this point, she didn't know what else to do but pray.

Nothing else to do BUT pray, she chided herself. Prayer is the ONLY thing powerful enough to bring a change in Jason's life, and I'm treating it like it's the last resort.

"Forgive me, Lord," Glenda prayed. Her heart whispered back, *Baby steps, baby steps . . .*

Are you trusting God one baby step at a time?

Prayer is weakness leaning on omnipotence.

God's Word vaults across the skies from
sunrise to sunset, melting ice, scorching
deserts, warming hearts to faith.

"Give, and it will be given to you. A good
measure, pressed down, shaken together and
running over, will be poured into your lap.
For with the measure you use,
it will be measured to you."

Whosoever shall give you a cup of water to drink
in my name, because ye belong to Christ, verily
I say unto you, he shall not lose his reward.

*Self-sacrifice is never
entirely unselfish, for the
giver never fails to receive.*

More than Words

Shannon rolled over in bed and labored to make out the numbers on the clock. "S . . . ?" she mumbled. "No, that's a five—five o'clock." She sat up, then shuffled across the cold wood floor into the bathroom.

"It's too early and too cold," she said to her haggard reflection in the bathroom mirror. She had to be at the homeless shelter in less than an hour to serve breakfast. *Why in the world did I volunteer for the early shift?* she wondered.

But as Shannon left the house, with her husband and children snuggled in their warm beds, she was startled and delighted by the sight before her. The most incredible sunrise—brimming over with purples, pinks, yellows, and oranges—swirled in the clouds above the mountains. Suddenly, the cold wasn't so cold anymore, and the early hour was inconsequential. It was as if God had painted that beautiful scene just for her.

When you give to others, you give to God, and He always returns the favor.

Guide me in your truth
and teach me.

PSALM 25:5

O Lord, You are my light!
You make my darkness bright.

2 SAMUEL 22:29 TLB

Call unto me, and I will answer thee,
and show thee great and mighty things,
which thou knowest not.

JEREMIAH 33:3 KJV

A Change for the Best

Megan knew the company needed help. If things didn't change soon, they'd all be out of a job. And with three kids in high school that wasn't an option for her. She had an idea, but it meant a major change in procedure, and her boss, Mr. Perkins, wasn't one who liked change. Megan wanted to present her plan at the staff meeting, but she was afraid Mr. Perkins would feel personally attacked. She knew the changes would work, but she wasn't sure where to go. So, she went to God.

The Bible didn't seem to give any definite answers about what she should do. But after praying, she felt she should set up an initial meeting with her boss to discuss her ideas. She'd take the next step after she saw how Mr. Perkins responded— and after she'd prayed about it again.

When the answers to your questions aren't black-and-white, God can help you sift through the gray. Don't hesitate to take a few moments and ask for His advice.

God shall be my hope, my stay, my guide, and lantern to my feet.

Worship the Lord
with the beauty of holy lives.

PSALM 96:9 TLB

I will bless the Lord at all times;
His praise shall continually
be in my mouth.

PSALM 34:1 NKJV

So through Jesus let us always
offer to God our sacrifice of praise,
coming from lips that speak his name.

HEBREWS 13:15 NCV

Sunday Service

It was a miracle—at least every parent of a preschooler attending Community Church was certain it was. Each week after the service, when parents went to pick up their kids from Sunday school, they found them sitting in a circle around Mrs. Harris, talking to God. Some parents even joked that their kids had a stronger prayer life than they did. But whenever anyone asked Mrs. Harris her secret, she simply said, "Kids like to talk, and God likes to listen."

Mrs. Harris made it into the adult service only once every few weeks, but her Sundays never lacked a time of worship. The time she spent with "her" kids, telling them all of the amazing things God had done and how very much He loved each one of them, was as much an act of worship as singing her favorite hymns.

True worship comes from the heart. Have you worshipped God today?

This is adoration: not a difficult religious exercise, but an attitude of the soul.

I know that my Redeemer lives.

JOB 19:25

We walk by faith, not by sight.

2 CORINTHIANS 5:7 KJV

What is faith? It is the confident
assurance that something we want is
going to happen. It is the certainty
that what we hope for is waiting for us,
even though we cannot see it up ahead.

HEBREWS 11:1 TLB

*What is faith, unless it is to believe
what you do not see?*

Glimpses in the Garden

Paula kicked about three pounds of mud off her boots and sat on the rotting wooden storage box. She loved the springtime. There was something satisfying about planting a garden and feeding her family from it. She didn't like the torrential rains, though. It was interesting that one of the most-needed ingredients for a successful garden—water—could also be its greatest enemy.

Somewhere beneath the mud and mulch, tiny green stems and leaves were gently unfolding. Though unseen, Paula knew they were straining to reach the surface and meet the sun's rays for the first time.

Between thunderclaps, it suddenly hit her. *I see new life every spring in this garden,* she thought. *I trust plants will grow even though I can't see them.* She recalled how Noah had trusted God even when others laughed at him. As a rainbow appeared in the distance, she decided it was time to trust God's unseen hand in all the areas of her life.

God's unseen hand is moving in your life as well.

He who watches over you will not slumber.

PSALM 121:3

My flesh and my heart fail;
but God is the strength of my
heart and my portion forever.

PSALM 73:26 NKJV

"I am the Lord, and I do not change."

MALACHI 3:6 NLT

No Rest for the Weary

Gena slumped into her chair, and her weary eyes closed. It was deadline day. Deadline night, actually. In just a few short hours, the article she had promised would be done "this Monday—absolutely it will be done Monday morning" would be due to the publisher. Luckily the kids spent the night at their grandparents' home.

The sudden landing of a large black-and-white cat in her lap snapped Gena to attention. "Hmm . . . thanks, Pepper. I guess I fell asleep again." Letter by letter, word by word, she forged ahead with her article. She quietly noted the irony of falling asleep while writing about a woman who had stayed awake for forty-eight hours straight to earn money for a local charity.

"There. Finished." She dared not look at the clock. As she shuffled off to bed, she thanked God for sleep. And then she paused. "You don't get to sleep, do You?" she asked. Then she smiled and said, "I guess someone has to tell the cats when to jump."

Let God be part of your late nights and early mornings.

Whether invoked or not, God will be present.

In return for my friendship
they accuse me,
but I am a man of prayer.

PSALM 109:4

May integrity and honesty protect me,
for I put my hope in You.

PSALM 25:21 NLT

Put on the new nature,
created after the likeness of God
in true righteousness and holiness.

EPHESIANS 4:24 RSV

Exercising Godliness

They called themselves "Phantom Five," and the staff at the gym nicknamed them "The Juice Girls." Although they couldn't sing a note, their language sure spiced up the workout room. Ellen could tell they were proud to be a part of the team that added spice to life at the gym in the morning. But things were getting out of hand. She was on the bike next to them when she said to one of them, "Hey, real ladies don't have to talk that way." She didn't want the frowns she got, but she smiled in a friendly way and continued her exercise.

She noticed that one girl, about the age of her daughter, had stopped hanging out with the group. *Hmmm,* she thought. *God might be up to something.* She prayed for the girl whenever she saw her and smiled when they passed each other.

Then one day, Ellen noticed the girl working out on the bike again. She smiled at her, and the girl came over. "I think you know something I need to know," she said to Ellen. "I can feel something different from you."

Do you speak up for what is right?

A man shows his character by what he laughs at.

39

He does not ignore
the cry of the afflicted.

PSALM 9:12

Their prayer offered in faith will heal the sick,
and the Lord will make them well.

JAMES 5:15 NLT

Heal me, O Lord, and I shall be healed;
save me, and I shall be saved:
for thou art my praise.

JEREMIAH 17:14 KJV

*How happy a person is depends
on the depths of his gratitude.*

Sick Day

It was only the stomach flu, but Lisa was sure she was at death's door. She hadn't taken a sick day for as long as she could remember. Even colds seemed to pass her by. But wherever this bug had come from, it had scored a direct hit.

Lisa's son tiptoed into her room, timidly bearing a cup of ice chips. "I'm praying for you, Mommy," he said, with a grown-up look of concern. Lisa smiled. Not only did the thought of her son's earnest prayer cheer her, but it also filled her with thanks. She realized how easy it was to take her good health for granted. It was a gift, and it was one Lisa would appreciate more earnestly thereafter.

If you have been blessed with good health, lift your voice and thank God. Then pray for someone you know who is struggling to overcome an illness. Thankfulness is a good way to strengthen your immune system.

Say only what helps, each word a gift.

EPHESIANS 4:29 THE MESSAGE

Exhort one another daily, while it is
called "Today," lest any of you be
hardened through the deceitfulness of sin.

HEBREWS 3:13 NKJV

Preach the word, be urgent in season
and out of season, convince, rebuke,
and exhort, be unfailing in
patience and in teaching.

2 TIMOTHY 4:2 RSV

Carefully Chosen Words

Meredith sorted through responses she could give to Ned's presentation. "Your idea is brilliant!" No, that would be a lie—and a mistake for the advertising firm. "I hate your idea." No, that would be too harsh. "My fourteen-year-old could have done a better job." Too snide. Besides, she would want someone to treat her son with respect and care if he were Ned.

"Ned, you clearly have a grasp of the general concept, but your execution went awry somewhere. I'd like to see you try again. Let's see if you can land closer to the client's wishes." Ned's excitement faded, but he agreed to try again.

Two weeks later, Ned returned to Meredith's office with a nearly flawless presentation. "I know now how off target my previous work was," he said as he packed up the storyboards. "Thanks for giving me another chance—and for not slamming the previous presentation as hard as it deserved. Your patience helped build my confidence."

Words are born in the heart, not in the head.

Are your words arrows that kill or arrows that point others in the right direction?

You made both summer and winter.

PSALM 74:17

The Lord will guide you continually,
and satisfy your desire with good things,
and make your bones strong; and you
shall be like a watered garden, like a
spring of water, whose waters fail not.

ISAIAH 58:11 RSV

He lets me rest in green meadows;
he leads me beside peaceful streams.

PSALM 23:2 NLT

The Promise of Spring

Andrea taped closed another moving box. "At least you don't have to pack every time you move south for the winter!" she barked at the robin perched outside the window. The kids giggled at their mom yelling at a bird. When Paul's company had downsized, salaries were cut. That forced their family to downsize from the home in the suburbs to a duplex close to the city. *God just isn't fair,* Andrea thought.

As she went to tape shut the final moving box, she caught sight of a framed photograph. There stood her family in front of their new home. She remembered how they'd thanked God for providing such an unexpected gift. That was ten years ago. *Paul still has his job, and we have our family,* thought Andrea. *Perhaps God hasn't been so unfair after all.* Maybe this was a season for appreciating what was truly valuable.

When life's circumstances make you feel as if it's the dead of winter, take comfort in knowing that seasons change. What season do you feel like you're in right now? What is God showing you through it?

> God wets you with His rain, but He also dries you with His sun.

Honor God with everything you own;
give him the first and the best.

PROVERBS 3:9 THE MESSAGE

We brought nothing into the world,
so we can take nothing out.

1 TIMOTHY 6:7 NCV

All day long the wicked covets, but the
righteous gives and does not hold back.

PROVERBS 21:26 RSV

We make a living by what we get,
but we make a life by what we give.

Hold On Loosely

I ris held tightly onto everything she owned. It was her money, right? Sure, she gave to the church, to charities, to others if there was anything left after bills, groceries, the children's clothing, and entertainment funds had been allocated.

Then one Sunday, Iris heard her pastor say, "Everything we own is God's. We're just caretakers." That bothered her. She liked having control over her money and her belongings. *Why does God need my money anyway?* she thought.

A few days later, Iris went to her favorite restaurant for dinner. When she asked for the "best steak you have," the waiter looked straight into her eyes and said, "I'm sorry, ma'am; we eat those in the back. We serve only what's left to customers." It took a moment to realize he was kidding, but suddenly the pastor's Sunday message made sense. During dessert, she began reworking her budget. She would give to God first—and give Him her best.

Does God get your best?

He will bless those who fear the Lord—
small and great alike.

PSALM 115:13

Never let loyalty and kindness get away
from you! Wear them like a necklace;
write them deep within your heart.
Then you will find favor with both God and
people, and you will gain a good reputation.

PROVERBS 3:3-4 NLT

Whenhe was in affliction, he besought
the Lord his God, and humbled himself
greatly before the God of his fathers.

2 CHRONICLES 33:12 KJV

A Place of Equality

Having the President of the United States visit Shelby's hometown was an unexpected pleasure—and inconvenience. There was a parade to be organized, security issues to be enforced, and proper honors to be bestowed. As the long-standing local mayor, Shelby was a rather important person in these parts. At least she'd felt that way until today. *The only perk being mayor has ever gotten me is a free cup of coffee at Greta's Diner,* she grumbled. *Even my kids are celebrity crazy today.*

At the luncheon, the president offered a blessing for the food, and that was when something dawned on Shelby. When he spoke to God, the president didn't have a higher place of honor than Shelby did. God didn't answer the president's prayer requests any faster than he did Shelby's. He didn't love him any more. In God's eyes, Shelby and the president held equal places of honor and blessing.

You are an important person in God's eyes too!

> *When God measures a person, He puts the tape around the heart, not the head.*

49

As high as the heavens are above the earth,
so great is his love for those who fear him.

PSALM 103:11

Who gives justice to the oppressed
and food to the hungry. The Lord
frees the prisoners. The Lord opens
the eyes of the blind. The Lord lifts
the burdens of those bent beneath
their loads. The Lord loves the righteous.

PSALM 146:7-8 NLT

The Lord your God is with you;
the mighty One will save you. He will
rejoice over you. You will rest in his love;
he will sing and be joyful about you.

ZEPHANIAH 3:17 NCV

Keep Looking Up

A kitten. A sports car. A dragon with a beard. Allison knew her son, Jake, loved to find pictures in the clouds. But she knew that looking up into a sky that seemed to go on forever always left Jake feeling smaller than he already knew he was.

"Jake," Allison asked one day, "is anything bigger than the sky?" Jake thought for a moment. The oceans were big, but he didn't think they were bigger. The mountains were tall, but you could tell where they ended. He knew that what he called the "sky" went farther than he could see— past the planets and beyond where anyone had ever gone before. "Nope," he said. He couldn't think of one thing that was bigger than it.

Allison smiled and said, "God's love for you is even bigger than the sky." Jake's eyes grew big with wonder. *Point made,* Allison thought.

Anytime you're feeling small or insignificant, look up. The sky is a reminder of a love too big to be measured.

God's love for us is proclaimed with each sunrise.

In his heart a man plans his course,
but the Lord determines his steps.

PROVERBS 16:9

Stalwart walks in step with God;
his path blazed by God, he's happy.

PSALM 37:23 THE MESSAGE

The Lord says, "I will guide you
along the best pathway for your life.
I will advise you and watch over you."

PSALM 32:8 NLT

Opportunities are seldom labeled.

Course Correction

Though Jenna's promotion was within striking distance, one thing stood in the way: Anna. Anna hadn't been there long, but she was talented, well-connected, and single without children. Jenna knew she'd done all she could to impress the boss, but tension between them remained because of her decision to put her husband and children before her job.

"Thanks for coming up to talk with me, Jenna," Mr. Thatcher began. "You've done great work for us; however, we're experiencing an unexpected downturn, and I'm afraid . . ."

Jenna didn't hear the rest of her soon-to-be former boss's words. She was still in shock a week later when Anna called her at home. She was starting a new company—seems she'd been downsized too. "We'd make a great team," she offered. Jenna thought about the time she'd put into getting a promotion and marveled that it had taken just one intervention from God to place this new opportunity in her path.

Do you need opportunities? God is more than able to guide your steps.

He set the earth on its foundations;
it can never be moved.

PSALM 104:5

"Fear not, for I am with you, be
not dismayed, for I am your God;
I will strengthen you, I will help you, I will
uphold you with my victorious right hand."

ISAIAH 41:10 RSV

The Lord is a strong fortress.
The godly run to him and are safe.

PROVERBS 18:10 TLB

Now That's Power

Martha admired the newest location of Samantha's dollhouse. Today, it sat on the hot-pink beanbag chair. Sam didn't seem to mind that the furniture had all shifted to the back. "Where are you going to move it tomorrow, honey?" Martha inquired.

"Don't know. Maybe the top bunk," Sam responded. That would be seventeen moves—only nine more than Martha and Sam had endured in real life over the last four years.

"I don't know the meaning of stability," Martha had joked with her neighbor Mrs. Olson.

"Well, I've moved twenty-seven times," Mrs. Olson had responded, "and I knew stability through each of those moves because God moved with us every time." That was six months ago. Martha and Sam were moving again next week. But thanks to Mrs. Olson and the seeds of their growing faith, she was sure this move would be the easiest one yet.

Are you searching for stability in your life? Look to the One who is always the same and who is always there.

All but God is changing day by day.

Teach us to number our days aright,
that we may gain a heart of wisdom.

PSALM 90:12

You saw me before I was born.
Every day of my life was recorded in
your book. Every moment was laid out
before a single day had passed.

PSALM 139:16 NLT

I consider that the sufferings of
this present time are not worthy
to be compared with the glory
which shall be revealed in us.

ROMANS 8:18 NKJV

Keeping Score

Vivian glanced across the bar and looked at her grown sons, Mike and Rick, planted in front of her TV watching the football game. They both loved football and were shouting, laughing, snacking, and having a good time. But Vivian knew there was a big difference between the two men and what they were doing.

For Mike, the game represented a time to relax and enjoy the company of a friend. But for Rick, football was more. He used it as an escape, not just from the stress of work, but also from his family and responsibilities. It was a convenient excuse he extended beyond football season to baseball, basketball, WWF wrestling, and anything else he could find on the sports channel.

Every life has a final buzzer. Thanks to grace, God doesn't keep track of points, fouls, and losses. But there's honor and reward in this life in the way we choose to invest our time. What about you? How are you using the time God has given you here on earth?

Life has no instant replays.

Lord, when doubts fill my mind,
when my heart is in turmoil, quiet me
and give me renewed hope and cheer.

PSALM 94:19 TLB

Cast your cares on the Lord and
he will sustain you; he will never
let the righteous fall.

PSALM 55:22

The sufferings of Christ abound in us, so our
consolation also abounds through Christ.

2 CORINTHIANS 1:5 NKJV

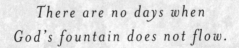

*There are no days when
God's fountain does not flow.*

Simple Miracles

"**M**y little butterfly." That's what Evelyn nicknamed her granddaughter Evie because she was constantly flitting here and there. One moment, she was a ballerina, the next, a snowflake. But after her daughter and son-in-law divorced, she saw Evie infrequently. The breakdown of her daughter's marriage was hard enough, but the loss of Evie was a heartache that seemed insurmountable. "Lord, I miss her and my daughter so much," Evelyn prayed. "How do I love them and let them go at the same time?"

The dog scratching at the back door interrupted her prayer. But as Evelyn opened the door, her heart filled with praise and wonder. The tree in the center of the yard was covered with butterflies. It seemed as if they waited only long enough for her to notice them before flying off in a colorful cloud of fluttering wings.

God's comfort can arrive in unexpected ways. Have you felt God's presence in an unexpected way that gave you a renewed sense of hope and cheer? Hang on to that wonderful experience.

our God for ever and ever;
he will be our guide even to the end.

PSALM 48:14

❧

"Truly, truly, I say to you, he who hears my
word and believes him who sent me, has
eternal life; he does not come into judgment,
but has passed from death into life."

JOHN 5:24 RSV

❧

The Lord shall reign forever and ever.

EXODUS 15:18 NKJV

❧

How Big Is Forever?

Sean always asked one question at the end of the bedtime story. Usually it was something like, "Are heffalumps real?" or "Can cats really wear hats and do all that stuff?" But tonight, Sean reached back and pulled out a tough one. "How big is forever?" Helen wondered how she could explain such a big concept to such a small boy.

"What do you think?" Redirection was always a good opening move—and a good way to buy time.

After a long pause, Sean answered. "I think it's almost as big as God."

Helen smiled. "I think you're probably right. You're the smartest boy I know. Good night, my angel." As she turned out the light, she marveled at her son's wisdom.

"Mom, can I ask one more question?" Helen stopped. "How long are we gonna be with Jesus in Heaven?" Helen smiled again.

"That's an easy one, Sean. Forever. Good night again."

When ten thousand times ten thousand times ten thousand years have passed, eternity will have just begun.

Every good promise of the
Lord your God has come true.

JOSHUA 23:15

"My grace is sufficient for you, for
My strength is made perfect in weakness."

2 CORINTHIANS 12:9 NKJV

Trust the Lord! Be brave and
strong and trust the Lord.

PSALM 27:14 CEV

Count on It

Karen marveled at April's resilience. April had lost a parent to cancer, a career to a downturn in the technology sector, good health to a serious case of the flu, and a purse to an unidentified subway assailant. That was just in the last six months. Having an infant during this time had put tremendous pressure on April.

"How do you stay so grounded—so balanced in the middle of all this terrible stuff?" Karen asked.

"I just hang on to God's promises." April said, as her baby girl cooed from the stroller.

Karen frowned. "You hang on to God's promises? What promises? That your life will fall apart all around you?"

April simply smiled. "No, I misspoke. I don't hang on to God's promises. I hold on to God's promise—singular, not plural."

"And what promise would that be?"

"That He would always be with me," April answered.

God's promise is for all those who will take hold of it. Will you?

Let a man go away or come back: God never leaves.

He determines the number of the stars
and calls them each by name.

PSALM 147:4

A good name is to be chosen
rather than great riches, loving favor
rather than silver and gold.

PROVERBS 22:1 NKJV

See what love the Father has
given us, that we should be called
children of God; and so we are.

1 JOHN 3:1 RSV

*What idea could we have
of God without the sky?*

What's in a Name?

Anya looked into the faces of her children when they were only moments old and wondered, *Is he a Paul, a Ryan, or more of a Sean? Is she a Rachel, a Beth, or a Katrina?* She chose their names with prayer for wisdom. She knew that names were God's way of guiding a person sometimes. He even renamed some people to show them how He saw them.

"Naming implies relationship," she told Paul, her husband, one night. "When we are close, we give each other nicknames. We name our pets and even our cars. But it would be strange if we named our new dishwasher or a log being placed on the fire because these are things to be used, not loved or named. And we love our children. So their names just have to be special, honey."

"So I take it Butch or Bruno is out?" Paul teasingly said. Anya laughed and threw a pillow at him.

If God feels each star is worthy of its own name, consider how much more He values you.

Before a word is on my tongue
you know it completely.

PSALM 139:4

A gentle response defuses anger, but
a sharp tongue kindles a temper-fire.

PROVERBS 15:1 THE MESSAGE

It is better to be patient than powerful;
it is better to have self-control
than to conquer a city.

PROVERBS 16:32 NLT

A Small Pause

Barb no longer had conversations with her teenage son, only arguments. Even a simple "Hi, how was your day?" was never really all that simple. The less communicative and more sullen Tyler became, the more Barb found herself exploding, saying things she'd never expected to hear coming out of her mouth. This morning, trying to get Tyler out of bed had sent her into a rage.

"If knowing God makes people act like you, you can keep it!" Tyler said bitterly, pulling the blankets back up over his head. Barb was struck speechless, and she quickly retreated to her room. She had a right to be angry, she argued, but what kind of impression had her angry words had on her son? She paused for a moment to ask God for the patience and wisdom she needed to deal with him. A peace came, and a creative idea—breakfast in bed. It worked!

Anger never produces positive change in others. Use your anger as a prayer alarm that tells you to ask God for help.

When anger enters the mind, wisdom departs.

Unless the Lord builds the house,
those who build it labor in vain.

PSALM 127:1 RSV

I leave you peace; my peace I give you.
I do not give it to you as the world does.
So don't let your hearts be troubled or afraid.

JOHN 14:27 NCV

The Lord is good,
a refuge in times of trouble.
He cares for those who trust in him.

NAHUM 1:7

Brandon Lane

Rachel used to enjoy driving down Brandon Lane. She had always imagined that the empty lot at the corner of Brandon Lane and Appletree would be the perfect spot to build her dream home. She'd had the plans for years. But somehow it hadn't happened.

A downturn in the economy had forced Rachel to cut back from a full-time job to a part-time job. The lot that once represented an exciting dream now seemed to speak only of disappointment.

Today she pulled her car up to the curb adjacent to the lot. With her daughter, Hannah, sleeping in her car seat, she bowed her head and released her dream to God. From that day on, she would let God lead the way, whether that meant a new home at the corner of Brandon Lane and Appletree or not. Either way, it was in God's hands. Rachel relaxed for the first time in many months. Now she could enjoy driving down Brandon Lane again.

If God shuts one door, He opens another.

Give your dreams to God. They're safe with Him.

Do not conform any longer to the
pattern of this world, but be transformed
by the renewing of your mind.

ROMANS 12:2

Yes, if you want better insight and discernment,
and are searching for them as you would for
lost money or hidden treasure, then wisdom
will be given you, and knowledge of God
himself; you will soon learn the importance of
reverence for the Lord and of trusting Him.
For the Lord grants wisdom! His every word is
a treasure of knowledge and understanding.

PROVERBS 2:3-7 TLB

According as his divine power hath given
unto us all things that pertain unto life
and godliness, through the knowledge of
him that hath called us to glory and virtue.

2 PETER 1:3 KJV

*Virtue is a state of war, and to
live in it we have always
to combat with ourselves.*

The "Don't Keep" Pile

"Kel, remember this one?" Linda asked her daughter, holding up the LP. Dust swirled around the faded jacket and found its way to Linda's nose. She sneezed.

"Yeah, I remember that one," laughed Kelly. "It's nothing to sneeze at! But let's face it, Mom, we don't even have a record player anymore. It was definitely the 'don't keep' pile."

"I suppose so," Linda answered. She couldn't help thinking that this attic cleaning was similar to what was going on in their lives. Both she and Kelly had begun to see contradictions in their actions and beliefs. But they were working on it. They had asked God to help them see what they needed to put into the "don't keep" pile.

How about you? Have you allowed God to help you sort through the good and the bad in your life? Perhaps it's time to see if you need to move a few items from the "keep" to the "don't keep" pile.

I will lie down and sleep in peace,
for you alone, O Lord, make me
dwell in safety.

PSALM 4:8

He gives power to the tired and worn out,
and strength to the weak.

ISAIAH 40:29 TLB

"My presence shall go with thee,
and I will give thee rest."

EXODUS 33:14 KJV

Sweet Dreams

The scream came from Kyle's bedroom. "It was a hairy monster with big yellow teeth," he told his mother, Monique, through a combination of hiccups, sobs, and tears. "If I close my eyes, I know he'll come back and get me!"

Monique held him close and told him to close his eyes. Then she began to pray. "Dear God, we know You're bigger than any monster. We also know Your arms are big enough to hold Kyle all the way from Heaven right down here to his bed and keep him safe. Amen." Kyle fell asleep in his mother's arms—and God's.

Though the words may change, the nighttime prayers that calm children's hearts do the same thing for adults. Whether it's nightmares or just the worries of the day that steal a sense of peace while you sleep, God is just a prayer away.

Nor can we fall below the arms of God, however low it be we fall.

No mind has conceived what God has
prepared for those who love him.

1 CORINTHIANS 2:9

"If you don't even believe me when
I tell you about things that happen here
on earth, how can you possibly believe if
I tell you what is going on in heaven?"

JOHN 3:12 NLT

"Don't fear, little flock, because your
Father wants to give you the kingdom."

LUKE 12:32 NCV

Bigger Than I Imagined

Missy didn't know what to expect as they approached the clearing. The drive through the thick jungle had been spectacular enough to fill a case of photo albums. She was thankful she'd decided to bring her sixteen-year-old daughter, Melinda, along for the shoot. They'd already seen rhinos, giraffes, and even a pride of lions. Still, nothing could have prepared her for the awesome beauty that lay just beyond the jungle.

Coming through the clearing, Missy was the first to see the magnificent cliff wall. It rose hundreds of feet straight up—well into the clouds in an otherwise sun-filled sky. A rainbow-colored mist floated dreamily around them as they rolled to a stop and got out of the truck. No one spoke, for no words could describe the splendor of this sight. Missy forgot all about her photography equipment as she hugged Melinda tight. She was certain she was viewing a picture of Heaven, and she thought, *It's bigger than I imagined.* And she was thankful she could share a glimpse of God's goodness with Melinda. It was a moment they'd never forget.

How big is your picture of Heaven? Think bigger. No, bigger still.

Heaven is a place prepared for those who are prepared for it.

Nothing in all creation
is hidden from God's sight.

HEBREWS 4:13

Jesus Christ the same yesterday,
and today, and for ever.

HEBREWS 13:8 KJV

I am always with you;
you have held my hand.

PSALM 73:23 NCV

God is above, presiding;
beneath, sustaining; within, filling.

Seeing and Believing

Darlene had never ridden in a convertible before, except in her adolescent daydreams. But here she was riding in a sports car along the Hawaiian coastline with her family. She'd never felt closer to Heaven. As they rounded a tight corner, a sudden gust of wind flipped her son's baseball cap off his head—and over the cliff. Her husband quickly pulled over, but one look told them it was a lost cause.

Heaven only knows where that thing is now, Darlene muttered to herself as she surveyed the rocky shore. Suddenly, she was struck by the truth of what she'd said so flippantly. God *did* know—just like God knew where Darlene stood right now, not only physically, but also spiritually. A moment ago, the ocean seemed so limitless to Darlene. Now, it seemed small in comparison to a God who knew everything that lay beneath it.

God sees you today—you and everything about you. He sees you, and He loves you anyway.

How good and pleasant it is when
brothers live together in unity!

PSALM 133:1

Do not speak evil of
one another, brethren.

JAMES 4:11 NKJV

He who loves God should
love his brother also.

1 JOHN 4:21 RSV

Still Fighting?

Kenny and Kirk were at it again. The two boys were arguing over who would pay for dinner. Katie laughed at her sons. "You two haven't changed at all."

"What do you mean? Of course we've changed—right, Kirk?"

"No, she's right; we haven't changed at all." The arguing continued, though in obviously mocked tones.

"What was it we used to fight about anyway?" asked Kenny.

"Nothing, really. Or maybe it was everything," Kirk replied.

"It was everything," confirmed Katie. "You each wanted to be seen as the best—the smartest, fastest, anything-est. All that competing, and look who ended up on top." Kirk flexed his muscles, and Kenny pointed at himself dramatically.

"Me!" Katie said, grabbing up the dinner check. After momentary stunned expressions, the threesome once again burst into laughter. *I'm lucky to have such a great family,* they each thought silently. *God has been good to us.*

Unity creates strength.

I will go before
you and
will level the
mountains.

ISAIAH 45:2

79

He does not fear bad news, nor
live in dread of what may happen.
For he is settled in his mind that
Jehovah will take care of him.

PSALM 112:7 TLB

Be strong and of good courage, do not
fear nor be afraid of them; for the Lord
your God, He is the One who goes with you.
He will not leave you nor forsake you.

DEUTERONOMY 31:6 NKJV

Facing Giants

They stood ten feet tall. No, taller. An impenetrable fortress. Cindy stood to give her presentation. The wall of suits neither moved nor spoke. At first, she stumbled over even the easiest words, but her confidence grew with every new page and every click of the remote.

After thirty minutes, she said, "Thank you for your consideration of this project." With those words she sat, certain her battle with the giants could have been waged no better. Did they notice the pauses? She hoped they had been viewed as effective tools for letting the ideas sink in, but in reality she knew they had been moments for impassioned and specific prayer.

It was up to the board of directors now. She wouldn't know for another week if her proposal had been accepted, but that didn't matter. She'd already beaten the giants— she'd overcome her fears in facing them. Cody, her teenaged son, had told her she could, and she did. She could thank God for that.

To help you face giants, God puts you on His shoulders.

How do you handle the giants in your path?

Along unfamiliar paths I will guide them;
I will turn the darkness into light before
them and make the rough places smooth.

ISAIAH 42:16

He led forth his people like sheep, and
guided them in the wilderness like a flock.

PSALM 78:52 RSV

"When the Holy Spirit, who is truth,
comes, he shall guide you into all truth,
for he will not be presenting his own ideas,
but will be passing on to you what he has
heard. He will tell you about the future."

JOHN 16:13 TLB

*Life is a lot like tennis—the one
who can serve best seldom loses.*

Obstacle Course

After Rebecca's children grew up and moved away, she accepted a position as youth leader. She loved working with teenagers. Their spiritual depth and immense love for God amazed her. Each year when the seniors graduated, she always felt some loss. Yet she also felt a sense of accomplishment. God had used her to help hundreds of young people grow. Then one day, Rebecca felt it was time to move closer to her grandchildren in another state.

On her last day as youth director, she was perplexed to discover the youth room had been turned into a huge, life-size maze. A blindfold with her name on it hung from the doorknob. She put it on and began to feel her way around the maze.

"Turn right," said one voice.

"Crawl under the table," said another. Familiar voices guided her step-by-step to the end.

As she rounded the final corner, she removed the blindfold. One hundred teenagers and young adults cheered and hugged her. Nineteen-year-old Meg finally answered the riddle of the maze. "We wanted to help you like you've helped us."

Never be afraid to invest into the lives of others what you have learned.

The Lord will provide.

GENESIS 22:14

God is able to make all grace abound
toward you, that you, always having
all sufficiency in all things, may have
an abundance for every good work.

2 CORINTHIANS 9:8 NKJV

I know how to live on almost nothing
or with everything. I have learned
the secret of living in every situation,
whether it is with a full stomach
or empty, with plenty or little.

PHILIPPIANS 4:12 NLT

Empty

To say "The cupboards were bare" would have been an understatement. Not only was there no food in the cupboards, but the cupboards themselves had long since fallen off the wall. They sat scattered around the cramped kitchen like box-shaped gnomes guarding the torn wallpapered walls.

"Bernie said he'd stop by today. I guess Debbie baked a cake she wants us to try," Cathy said, as she tried to smile.

"Oh, come on. It'll be fine," Lester encouraged. "We just need to make it until next month. They promised to send the insurance check by then."

"I know. It's just that a piece of cake is the last thing we need right now."

A knock on the door interrupted their conversation. "Bernie . . . Debbie? What's all this?" Cathy asked in surprise. Bernie just smiled. And within minutes, the kitchen was filled with boxes of food and supplies. The kids squealed with delight at the sight of cake and pudding mixes. When everything had been unloaded, the friends bowed their heads and thanked God for His provision.

God's investment in us is so great He could not possibly abandon us.

Change your mind and attitude
to God and turn to him so he can
cleanse away your sins and send
you wonderful times of refreshment
from the presence of the Lord.

ACTS 3:19 TLB

If they obey and serve him, they will
spend the rest of their days in prosperity
and their years in contentment.

JOB 36:11

To the man who pleases Him
God gives wisdom and knowledge and joy.

ECCLESIASTES 2:26 RSV

Inside Job

Felicia was a good moral woman. She didn't cheat on her husband, kick the dog, or belittle her children. She had a prestigious job, a nice house with a reasonable mortgage, and a personal trainer. Family, friends, and business associates all felt that she was an all-around great person.

So after she committed her life to God, those around her didn't notice much of a difference on the outside. But on the inside, Felicia felt as though she'd been sleepwalking through her entire life. At last, she felt fully awake, fully alive.

God's presence in your life can bring about dramatic changes. It can revitalize relationships, break destructive habits, even give you a renewed sense of purpose. But there are also day-to-day blessings, times of refreshment, and joy that seem to spring up out of nowhere. Don't get so busy with your daily agenda that you miss them.

The glory of God is a person fully alive.

He who dwells in the shelter of the Most High
will rest in the shadow of the Almighty.

PSALM 91:1

He restores my soul.

PSALM 23:3 RSV

I will seek that which was lost, and bring
again that which was driven away, and will
bind up that which was broken, and
will strengthen that which was sick.

EZEKIEL 34:16 KJV

*God's presence is a vacation
destination that requires
no reservations!*

Rendezvous

Wendy moved her beach towel from the scorching sands to the shade of a lone palm tree and surveyed the beach, her eyes stopping on each of her children playing in the sand. On this long-awaited vacation, rest was high on her agenda, but feeling like the main course at a barbecue was not. As she dozed in the comfort of the shade, lulled by the rhythmic sound of the waves, she felt God's presence. Wendy basked in it, like a long hug from an old friend.

Just being with someone you love, and who loves you in return, feels a bit like a vacation. There's comfort in knowing you're more than accepted; you're cherished. You can rest in being who you really are, without any pretense or expectations.

When was the last time you scheduled a vacation with God? Some call it meditation or a retreat. What you call it isn't as important as actually doing it. Whether it lasts a few minutes or a matter of days, time spent with the One you love is never wasted.

"Where two or three are gathered
together in My name, I am there
in the midst of them."

MATTHEW 18:20 NKJV

The eyes of the Lord are upon
the righteous, and his ears
are open to their prayers.

1 PETER 3:12 RSV

As iron sharpens iron, so people
can improve each other.

PROVERBS 27:17 NCV

Group Effort

After sending her husband to work and children to school, Sue expected the phone to ring at precisely 8:45, just as it did every weekday morning. Sue answered, "G'morning, Janelle!" After a few minutes of pleasantries, the two got down to the business at hand. Even though their schedules kept them from meeting face-to-face very often, their time of prayer brought them closer to each other and to God. It was a habit that both of them had no desire to break.

Corporate prayer may sound like a business enterprise, but it's really more like a conference call to God. It can be two friends praying over lunch or a congregation joining with the heart of their pastor as he prays aloud for their city. It can be silent or spoken, even recited in unison.

The next time you pray in a group, why not set up an extra chair to remind you that the God of the universe is right there beside you, joining in?

Friends that pray together stay together.

He is before all things,
and in him all things hold together.

COLOSSIANS 1:17

"Don't be afraid, for I am with you.
Do not be dismayed, for I am your God.
I will strengthen you. I will help you. I will
uphold you with my victorious right hand."

ISAIAH 41:10 NLT

The Lord shall preserve you from all evil,
He shall preserve your soul. The Lord shall
preserve your going out and your coming in
from this time forth, and even forevermore.

PSALM 121:7-8 NKJV

Whole Again

It was only a slow leak. But after a few weeks, the cabinets under the kitchen sink looked like a swamp. Janie thought that all Carl would have to do was tighten the pipe. Now, the kitchen had all the makings of a Titanic sequel. Janie kept the boys out of the kitchen while Carl hurried to the garage and grabbed his secret weapon.

"At least it'll hold until I can get a plumber out here," Carl told her, as he unrolled foot after foot of duct tape around the ailing plumbing. Once the deluge was back to its original trickle, Janie looked at Carl's work with pride.

This stuff can hold anything together, she chuckled to herself. *Kinda like what God does for me, every time my life goes on the fritz.*

God is much more than cosmic duct tape. He doesn't just patch up your life; He gives you a new one. Are there any leaky areas in your life that need God's healing touch?

Ignoring a leak may be inviting a flood.

He puts a little of heaven in our hearts
so that we'll never settle for less.

2 CORINTHIANS 5:5 THE MESSAGE

"If I go and prepare a place for you,
I will come again, and receive you unto myself;
that where I am, there ye shall be also."

JOHN 14:3 KJV

"I tell you the truth, whoever
believes has eternal life."

JOHN 6:47 NCV

*The one who thinks most of
Heaven will do most for earth.*

The Best Is Yet to Come

The dryer buzzer echoed throughout the house, awakening the baby who'd only moments before finally fallen into a fitful sleep. Sharon began folding her fifth load of laundry, hoping the baby would return to his nap. The floors still needed scrubbing, and she hadn't made it to the grocery store. The chores never ended.

Sharon didn't want to complain. After all, she had a nice house, a good husband, a healthy child, and an adequate grocery budget. Still, when she felt overwhelmed by the responsibilities and the work, she would take a few moments, sit back, and talk to God about Heaven. Those God moments renewed her perspective and filled her with a sense of peace and joy. *God is so good to me,* she thought.

Heaven on earth is only a fantasy, but God has something different planned for eternity. Why not spend some time with God, praising Him for the reality of Heaven?

How can I repay the Lord
for all his goodness to me?

PSALM 116:12

We should be well satisfied without money
if we have enough food and clothing.

1 TIMOTHY 6:8 TLB

My God will supply every need
of yours according to his riches
in glory in Christ Jesus.

PHILIPPIANS 4:19 RSV

Withdrawal Symptoms

It wasn't your typical glimpse of God. Ginger was paying bills. Usually, this time of the month was one of her least favorites. That comfortable cushion of savings she'd always planned to have just never seemed to materialize. And every time she got a raise, the bills just seemed to grow along with her income. There was always just barely enough to cover groceries, doctor bills, and her son's mouthful of braces.

Barely enough, but enough. This month, as Ginger wrote check after check, instead of getting more depressed, she found herself offering thanks to God. By the time she was finished, the pile of bills felt like a pile of blessings. After all, that's what her income was for, and God had given her all she needed for yet another month. That was a real reason for thanks.

Even when times are tight, there's still room to thank God for His provision. Why not turn the next bill you pay into a chance to praise God?

A grateful heart helps balance even the tightest budget.

In your unfailing love you will lead
the people you have redeemed.

Exodus 15:13

Give us help for the hard task;
human help is worthless.
In God we'll do our very best;
he'll flatten the opposition for good.

Psalm 60:11-12 The Message

All of us have sinned and fallen short
of God's glory. But God treats us
much better than we deserve, and
because of Christ Jesus, he freely
accepts us and sets us free from our sins.

Romans 3:23-24 CEV

Wrong Moves

The phone lines were buzzing. If Gina had to answer one more call about the ministry director's "fall from grace," she was going to switch everything over to the answering machine. Maybe she could just have Gordon record a message that said, "I'm sorry," over and over again. Then she could play it for whoever had a question.

Not that Gina didn't have questions of her own. She had a hard time believing any of this was really happening. Gordon was a good man, but he'd badly failed the people who'd put their trust in him. Yet, so many of those calling were voicing their disappointment in God, as though He'd been the One who'd failed. All Gina could say was, "God's really the only One you can trust not to fail."

Have the ungodly actions of someone you always considered godly ever caused you to doubt God's reality or power?

Trust lightly in men.
Trust heavily in God.

I spread out my hands to you;
my soul thirsts for you like a parched land.

PSALM 143:6

❦

In the day of my trouble I will call upon thee:
for thou wilt answer me.

PSALM 86:7 KJV

❦

The blessing of the Lord makes a person rich,
and He adds no sorrow with it.

PROVERBS 10:22 NLT

❦

*It takes prayer to bloom
where God plants you.*

Oasis

Silk was Marjorie's plant of choice. It's not that she didn't enjoy the beauty of a manicured garden or the scent of a fresh-cut rose; she just couldn't seem to keep anything with a root system alive. Marjorie knew she wasn't totally inept. Her children hung in there year after year. She never forgot to give them food or water, but plants just seemed to slip her mind. Until, of course, their brown shriveled leaves began falling onto the carpet.

Marjorie could relate. Lately, that was exactly what she felt like inside—shriveled and fragile, uncared for. She kept telling herself that her hectic schedule was only for a season, but the season never seemed to end. Being successful at work did nothing to quench the thirst she felt in her soul. She knew that was something God alone could do, so she bowed her head and asked God to fill her up. And He did.

Are you thirsting for something only God can give? Ask Him for what you need.

You bestow glory on me
and lift up my head.

PSALM 3:3

Though they stumble, they will not fall,
for the Lord holds them by the hand.

PSALM 37:24 NLT

Whatever is born of God overcomes
the world. And this is the victory that
has overcome the world—our faith.

1 JOHN 5:4 NKJV

Defeating Defeat

"You can do it!" "Knock it out of the park!" "Go! Go! Go!" As the batter came up to the plate, the cries from the crowd grew steadily into a roar. But one voice rose above them all, at least in Brandon's mind. The voice was that of his mother, Kay. "C'mon son, give it all you've got!"

Brandon swung—and missed. Strike three. The game was over, and the home team lost by a single run. Brandon pulled his cap down over his eyes and dejectedly walked back to his teammates. His mom and dad were already there, waiting with open arms.

"I'm so proud of you, Brandon," his dad said, as he knelt down to look him in the eye. Kay hugged him tightly, "You've practiced so hard since the last game. You just wait. Your day is coming."

You won't win every game in life. Sometimes, you won't even score. But when it comes to His children, God never misses a game.

It's better to strike out than sit on the sidelines.

Do not wear yourself out to get rich;
have the wisdom to show restraint.

PROVERBS 23:4

Do nothing from selfishness or conceit,
but in humility count others better
than yourselves. Let each of you look
not only to his own interests, but
also to the interests of others.

PHILIPPIANS 2:3-4 RSV

A house is built by wisdom and
becomes strong through good sense.
Through knowledge its rooms are filled with
all sorts of precious riches and valuables.

PROVERBS 24:3-4 NLT

Fool's Gold

Carolyn sat up straight in bed, shaking. Her husband grumbled in his sleep and went back to snoring. It was a nightmare. She was in her living room, and a visitor picked up a picture frame off the bookcase with the comment, "Ahh! This is your treasure." He turned it towards her, and she expected to see a picture of her family.

Instead, it was a huge portrait of the nearest shopping mall! She awoke instantly with a tremendous feeling of embarrassment and awareness. "I'm sorry, God," she whispered. "I didn't realize how much things were beginning to mean to me. Please forgive me."

God stresses loving people, not possessions or position. Although one way of showing love is providing for your family, sacrificing your relationships to do it is rather counterproductive. Take a moment and talk to God about what role money plays in your life.

Sometimes, raising your standard of living means taking a cut in pay.

Let us not give up meeting together,
as some are in the habit of doing,
but let us encourage one another.

HEBREWS 10:25

Now go out and encourage your servants.

2 SAMUEL 19:7 NCV

Take delight in the Lord.

PSALM 37:4 NLT

The church is like a bank—
the more you put into it,
the more interest you have in it.

Playing Hooky

As the amusement park gates were locked behind her, Candy looked back on her Sunday with satisfaction. Roller coasters, Ferris wheels, flume rides, bumper cars—you name it, she loved them all. She started telling her husband how much more fun this was than sitting in church, but she stopped short. What kind of message was she sending her children?

Beyond what the kids would think, Candy began wondering what that comment said about her own relationship with God. She knew God didn't promise a burning bush every Sunday. But at the end of a tough workweek, Candy also felt as though she should be able to treat herself. What better treat than spending time with God was all she could think about the rest of the day.

The expectation of meeting with the living God should be about as exciting as life gets. But God isn't entertainment. He's comfort, conviction, joy, peace, power, and love in action. This Sunday, ask God to open your eyes and ears to the message He's prepared just for you. Then, act on it.

Once more I will astound these people
with wonder upon wonder.

ISAIAH 29:14

Yes, the gladness you have given me is
far greater than their joys at harvest time
as they gaze at their bountiful crops.

PSALM 4:7 TLB

Does the hawk take flight by your wisdom
and spread his wings toward the south?

JOB 39:26 NIV

Flight of Fancy

Janice taxied the private plane into the small county airport. It had been another perfect flight: great weather, beautiful scenery, and the joy of soaring above the hustle and bustle of life. Although she'd had her pilot's license for almost six months now, she never ceased to be amazed at the intricacy of a plane's instrumentation and design. *I can't imagine having a brain that could come up with something like this,* she thought.

At that exact moment, an ordinary gray-and-white pigeon flew past the cockpit window. Janice hardly would have noticed it on any other day, but today she looked at it through the eyes of a pilot. The bird had no instrumentation, yet it possessed such ease, beauty, and agility in flight. *Man's greatest creations can't hold a candle to God's simplest wonders,* she marveled. She took a moment to thank God for the beauty of His creation.

Have you thanked God for the beauty around you today?

God is an Artist, and creation, His gallery.

When words are many, sin is not absent,
but he who holds his tongue is wise.

PROVERBS 10:19

He who is slow to anger has
great understanding, but he
who has a hasty temper exalts folly.

PROVERBS 14:29 RSV

Don't sin by letting anger gain
control over you. Don't let the sun
go down while you are still angry.

EPHESIANS 4:26 NLT

Blizzard

Snowflakes pelted the windshield of Carla's van. It was hard to believe these small, inconsequential flakes would pile up into two-foot drifts by morning. But she had lived in the Rockies long enough to take storm warnings seriously. A blizzard was predicted, and she knew she was being foolish. Slowly, she took a deep breath and let her anger drain away.

The reason she was driving around in the first place was because of the bitter argument she'd had with her husband. She slammed out of the house before she could say even one more thing she'd regret in front of the children. She pictured her words piling up just like those snowflakes. One by one her angry words had become a whiteout. She stopped the van, prayed for a moment, and then turned the car around. With God's help, it was time to start shoveling.

Words are loaded pistols.

Have your words created a blizzard for someone you love? Perhaps it's time to start shoveling.

This is the day the Lord has made;
let us rejoice and be glad in it.

PSALM 118:24

Search for the Lord and for his strength,
and keep on searching. Think of the
wonderful work he has done, the miracles,
and the judgments he handed down.

1 CHRONICLES 16:11 NLT

All the days of the afflicted are evil,
but he who is of a merry heart
has a continual feast.

PROVERBS 15:15 NKJV

Life is a series of surprises.

365 Blessings a Year

The streamers were down, the gifts were opened and put away, and all that remained of the cake was a plateful of dry crumbs. Yesterday was Rhonda's fiftieth birthday, and today was—well—just another day. As she came home from work, Rhonda felt like a sad little kid at the end of summer vacation. "The party's over," she sighed. "Literally."

Downstairs, she heard the phone ring. "It's for you," her husband said.

The call came as a total surprise—"Mom?" It was her daughter in need of advice. They ended the call after a two-hour talk. "Thanks, Mom. I really needed to hear your voice. I love you." Rhonda's heart glowed. It was summer again.

She realized then that life would never be a boring rerun. She had things to do that only she could do. In that moment, she thanked God for all the tasks and adventures He had planned for her—especially the unexpected ones.

Look for the unexpected surprises God has placed in your path.

He rescued me because
he delighted in me.

PSALM 18:19

We love him, because he first loved us.

1 JOHN 4:19 KJV

By grace you have been saved
through faith; and this is not your
own doing, it is the gift of God.

EPHESIANS 2:8 RSV

Saving Grace

As Vivian prepared dinner, she absentmindedly listened to the six o'clock news. After the traffic update, a reporter interviewed a woman outside a burning apartment building. The elderly woman had risked her life to save her cat. "He's everything to me," she said breathlessly, clutching the animal tightly to her chest.

What a stupid thing to do! Vivian thought. She wondered about what would make her run back into a burning house. Her kids, of course. But what about her neighbor's kids? A vagrant? A mountain of cash? *I guess the more something matters to you, the more you're willing to risk saving it.* Then she thought, *I wonder who would feel I was worth saving?*

In that moment, she was reminded how God had rescued her from the prescription drug addiction that had been burning a hole in her soul. He had made her feel worth saving all right. It was good to be reminded.

God thinks you're worth saving. He's already proven it.

Crisis reveals where your true priorities lie.

The Lord is my light and my salvation;
Whom shall I fear?

PSALM 27:1 NKJV

Be of good courage, and
he shall strengthen your heart,
all ye that hope in the Lord.

PSALM 31:24 KJV

We should not be like cringing,
fearful slaves, but we should
behave like God's very own children,
adopted into the bosom of his family,
and calling to him, "Father, Father."

ROMANS 8:15 TLB

Eclipsing Fear

As the sky grew darker, Greta's mind returned to the first time she'd ever seen an eclipse. She was only six, but she still remembered the eerie feeling that came over her as the afternoon sun dimmed and a strange dusk overtook her neighborhood. Right now, in the middles of this eclipse, she was feeling that same fear once again.

Greta found herself pulling over to the side of the road to watch this amazing phenomenon. As she waited, she realized that her anxiety was not because the darkness appeared to be eating away at the sun, but because her fear of losing her daughter to her future son-in-law appeared to be eating away at her—even though she knew they were just right for each other, a precious gift from God. She leaned over the steering wheel and prayed for courage. In that moment, she remembered how much she loved her daughter, and she drove on to the wedding.

Are you letting the darkness swallow the light in your life?

Courage is fear that's said its prayers.

I have the desire to do what is good,
but I cannot carry it out. For what I do
is not the good I want to do; no, the evil
I do not want to do—this I keep on doing.

ROMANS 7:18-19

Commit your work to the Lord,
then it will succeed.

PROVERBS 16:3 TLB

He that hath no rule over his own spirit is like
a city that is broken down, and without walls.

PROVERBS 25:28 KJV

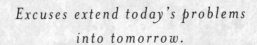

*Excuses extend today's problems
into tomorrow.*

Oops, I Did It Again

After three weeks, Nancy hadn't lost a pound of the weight her doctor had advised she lose before her surgery. "I've been exercising and have cut out snacking altogether," Nancy told her doctor. "I guess I just have a slow metabolism or something."

But to herself, Nancy carried on a totally different conversation. *I did get to the gym that once and worked out a really long time. I've just been so busy. I only have a bag of chips instead of those chocolate cupcakes I used to get.* She knew she was stretching the truth, but she just couldn't help it. She felt really guilty.

"Okay, Doc, I confess," she said. "The truth is, I blew it."

Her doctor just grinned and said, "I forgive you, but your recovery's going to be a little harder." Silently, Nancy prayed for more self-control and decided she wouldn't give up. She'd ask her family for help, something she found difficult to do. She would change—one moment at a time.

He has made everything
beautiful in its time.

ECCLESIASTES 3:11

Love the LORD, all you his saints!
The LORD preserves the faithful.

PSALMS 31:23 RSV

Take courage as you fulfill your duties.

2 CHRONICLES 19:11 NLT

Becoming

When Fiona took up the bagpipes, she thought it would be a way to connect with her ancestral heritage. Now it seemed more like a way to make enemies out of her neighbors. But things were looking up. The first week her children complained that "Amazing Grace" sounded like farm animals in a blender. By the end of the first month, there were a few recognizable notes amidst the more common squeaks and squawks.

And by the family reunion that next year, she was actually enjoying herself. Best of all, so were those who happened to be listening. "Fiona, you're a natural!" her aunt congratulated her. Her children were proud of her for her diligence.

Smiling, she remembered all those moments when she thought she'd never be able to get it right. Then she realized that she, too, was still a work in progress—an unfinished symphony—and she prayed God would continue to mold her into a masterpiece.

Have you given your talents to God? He has a masterpiece in mind for you as well.

Beauty isn't skin deep. It goes all the way to the heart.

God sets the lonely in families.

PSALM 68:6

Love never ends.

1 CORINTHIANS 13:8 NCV

Love suffers long and is kind.

1 CORINTHIANS 13:4 NKJV

Love and Loss

Holidays were always the hardest. Leigh had a wonderful family of her own, but she felt the keen loss of her parents. First it had been her father. It had been so hard watching him die of lung cancer ten years ago. Then this fall, her mother had died in her sleep.

Leigh's youngest daughter came bounding into the bedroom and gave her a big, wet kiss. "Merry Christmas, Mommy," she squealed. Leigh held her tightly, thanking God for the little girl in her arms. *If I didn't love so deeply, I guess good-byes wouldn't hurt so much,* she thought.

She followed her little daughter into the living room. Watching her tear open her presents, she thanked God that even when love is painful, it's worth every moment.

At times, it may be difficult to believe, but love and loss are two sides of the same coin. God in His wisdom allows for both.

It is love not reason, that is stronger than death.

"Who of you by worrying can
add a single hour to his life?"

MATTHEW 6:27

"Behold, God is my salvation;
I will trust, and will not be afraid;
for the Lord God is my strength and my
song, and He has become my salvation."

ISAIAH 12:2 RSV

The person who trusts in the
Lord will be blessed. The Lord will
show him that he can be trusted.

JEREMIAH 17:7 NCV

It is not work that kills men.
It is worry.

Not to Worry

It seemed that everywhere Becky turned these days, she saw warning signs. Since she announced she was pregnant, the world seemed like a more dangerous place. How could they raise a child in such a violent, polluted society? Flammable. Dangerous undertow. Non-potable water. Do not touch. Poisonous. Slippery when wet. Keep out of the hands of children! And now kids were shooting other kids in schools all over the country.

Watching her husband, John, sleep, Becky admitted her fear to God. "Lord, I'm so scared. What if we can't protect our child? What if I turn out to be a lousy mother? What if John loses his job? Or what if I die? What would John do then? Help me, Lord."

Gradually, an overwhelming love and peace filled her heart. All the good things of life flooded her mind—mountain meadows, the laughter of children, and the faces of friends and family. She realized God loved her unborn child even more than she did, and with that thought, she drifted off into a peaceful sleep.

Great is his faithfulness;
his lovingkindness begins afresh each day.

LAMENTATIONS 3:23 TLB

He is faithful and just to forgive us
our sins and to cleanse us
from all unrighteousness.

1 JOHN 1:9 NKJV

In him we have redemption through
his blood, the forgiveness of our
trespasses, according to the riches of
his grace which he lavished upon us.

EPHESIANS 1:7-8 RSV

Fresh Start

Annie woke up with a cloud hanging over her head. She shouldn't have said those things to the kids. They were just kids. "Forgive me, Father," she said. She sighed and got dressed. She still felt like God was angry.

Cory popped out of his room. "Hi, Mom!" He grinned and went into the bathroom.

"Mom!" Little Sarah ran up and hugged Annie's knees.

"Mommy's sorry about being so angry last night."

"It's okay," said Sarah. "You had a bad day. Can I have a bad day today? I can't find my doll."

Annie smiled through her tears. If her kids could forgive her, then maybe she should believe that God could too.

You can trust God never to hold a grudge. No matter what you did or said the night before, His forgiveness, healing, and love are waiting for you even before a new day has dawned.

The question is, are you willing to accept it?

God believes in you, even when you don't believe in Him.

"Come unto me, all ye that labor and are
heavy laden, and I will give you rest."

MATTHEW 11:28 KJV

My soul is feasted as with marrow and fat,
and my mouth praises thee with joyful lips,
when I think of thee upon my bed, and
meditate on thee in the watches of the night.

PSALM 63:5-6 RSV

The Lord shows his true love every day.
At night I have a song, and
I pray to my living God.

PSALM 42:8 NCV

Too Busy?

Another tough day and the kids were finally in bed. Sandra grabbed her bowl of popcorn and the TV remote, ready for an evening of relaxation. She surfed the channels on her big screen. Rerun . . . rerun . . . rerun. All she wanted was something new. She finally settled on the evening news. No reruns there—at least until 10 o'clock. But it was the same old stuff.

Finally, she just clicked off the TV and stared at the ceiling. *I bet there won't be any reruns in Heaven,* she thought, and then she laughed out loud. It had been awhile since she had thought about God. She'd been so busy; she hadn't had time for daily devotions. "Really?" She felt God ask her.

The truth was, she spent every evening watching mind-numbing TV to keep from thinking about the stress of the day. Maybe it was time she started talking to God instead.

God is waiting to ease your tired mind and relax your burdened soul.

Hurry is the death of prayer.

You who seek God, may your hearts live!

PSALM 69:32

God hath chosen the weak things
of the world to confound
the things which are mighty.

1 CORINTHIANS 1:27 KJV

We have this treasure from God,
but we are like clay jars that hold
the treasure. This shows that the
great power is from God, not from us.

2 CORINTHIANS 4:7 NCV

*If your life is in neutral,
prayer can shift it into gear.*

The Great Adventure

It wasn't that Christine was afraid to die. She completely believed in God's promise that there was something beyond this life. The hardest part of her life for her to accept was when events spun out of her control. Everyone who knew her knew how much she liked to have a "plan" for everything. From her vacations to setting her children's clothes out for school the next day, Christine's life was organized and predictable. That was just the way she liked it.

If the truth were told, there was only one thing that Christine was afraid of—to really live. Life was easiest for her when she knew what to expect. As the children grew, life became messy, uncontrollable, and risky. Last night her son, Michael, said, "Mom, life is an adventure. You're not supposed to know everything before it happens. Isn't there something you've always wanted to do? Stop sleepwalking your way through life."

It was a wake-up call for Christine—how about you? Will you give God control of your life and enjoy the adventure?

Surely you desire truth in
the inner parts; you teach me
wisdom in the inmost place.

PSALM 51:6

He makes known secrets that are deep
and hidden; he knows what is hidden
in darkness, and light is all around him.

DANIEL 2:22 NCV

Turn us again to yourself, O God.
Make your face shine down upon us.

PSALM 80:3 NLT

Unknown Territory

The darkness that loomed ahead felt like an unexplored cavern, dangerous and foreboding. Whitney squelched the impulse to turn back. She knew she couldn't put it off any longer. Hesitantly, she pushed the automatic door opener and flooded the garage with sunshine. The car no longer fit inside. Spring cleaning was long overdue.

Amid the empty cartons, broken sprinkler heads, and long-lost garden tools, Whitney found hidden treasure—the ballet slippers she wore during elementary school. "Thought I'd lost those three moves ago," she chuckled. She wondered if her own daughter would try out a pair of slippers soon. From that moment on, her chore turned into a treasure hunt.

In one box, she found a bundle of valentines from Steve that she'd kept from before they were married. With this last move, she had shut out everyone, including God. In that moment, she realized that if she were to ever start living again, she would need to open the windows and doors of her soul much like she'd opened the garage door.

Does God need to do some spring cleaning in your life?

What's hidden in your heart will be revealed in your life.

The sacrifices of God are a broken spirit;
a broken and contrite heart.

PSALM 51:17

He who sows sparingly will also
reap sparingly, and he who sows
bountifully will also reap bountifully.

2 CORINTHIANS 9:6 RSV

Take heed that you do not
do your charitable deeds
before men, to be seen by them.

MATTHEW 6:1 NKJV

Matters of the Heart

The house was quiet, except for the muffled sobs coming from the family room. If Tera's husband had seen her, she knew he would have been shocked. She was always under control. Her life seemed so balanced—so good. She was a hard-working mother who gave herself to her family and church work; and she was always generous, especially to those less fortunate.

But this morning as she prayed, Tera realized that her motivation for doing these things was not really love, but rather a desire to look good in the eyes of others. She did what was convenient and easy. If it happened to please God, that was an added benefit. But God wanted more than her time and money; He wanted her whole heart. And at last Tera knew she no longer wanted to hold it back from Him. Kneeling by her chair, she finally asked for God's forgiveness.

God wants your heart too— as soon as you're willing to give it to Him.

Repentance is the tear in the eye of faith.

"Love the Lord your God with
all your heart and with all your
soul and with all your mind."

MATTHEW 22:37

We have the mind of Christ.

1 CORINTHIANS 2:16 RSV

If any of you lacks wisdom, let him ask of
God, who gives to all liberally and without
reproach, and it will be given to him.

JAMES 1:5 NKJV

*God does not belong to the class of existing
things . . . not that he has no existence,
but that he is above all existing things,
nay even above existence itself.*

Everything You've Got

"You know, Michele, I find it difficult to connect with God intellectually," Emily said as she twirled the red-and-white straw in her son's leftover chocolate shake. The kids had headed to the game room.

"Heh?" Michele replied, reaching across the table to steal some fries from her daughter's plate.

"I mean, I have no problem accepting Him on an emotional level," she plunged forward as Michele eyed the rest of Emily's burger.

"Go ahead. I'm listening," Michele said as her friend pushed the burger fragment toward her.

"Anyway, I just have a hard time relating to God intellectually. Any ideas?" she looked at Michele, who was attempting to speak and swallow at the same time, and then she threw up her hands in disgust. "I'm trying to have an intellectually stimulating discussion with a complete bananahead." Then, suddenly, she understood. "That's it, Michele! I don't connect with God intellectually because I'm not on His level. Thanks."

"It's time to step up and speak to Him at your own level," Michele agreed.

How are you connecting with God?

Each of you must take responsibility
for doing the creative best
you can with your own life.

GALATIANS 6:5 THE MESSAGE

Be strong and courageous,
do not fear or be dismayed.

2 CHRONICLES 32:7 NKJV

In all these things we are more than
conquerors through him who loved us.

ROMANS 8:37 RSV

Short of Excellence

Diana and her husband, Mark, chose similar careers. Diana freelanced as an editor for a publishing house, while Mark wrote copy for an advertising firm. Each Wednesday they met for lunch at a small café just a few blocks from Mark's office. After talking about the kids' schoolwork and who got carpool duty that day, Mark talked about his work.

"You wouldn't believe the ad contract we just turned down. It would have been huge," Mark said. "But as we sat there in the planning meeting, it just didn't feel right. It was just one of those moments when I knew God was telling me not to do it. I know I could have lost my job, but I want to be proud of my work."

"I know you did the right thing," Diana responded. "You've got to follow God's level of excellence instead of the world's, not just for God but for the kids. They watch you."

Sometimes taking responsibility means giving something up.

Do your kids see you making decisions that are right and also that cost you something?

It pays to take life seriously;
things work out when you trust in God.

PROVERBS 16:20 THE MESSAGE

Be self-controlled and alert.

1 PETER 5:8

"Because your heart was tender,
and you humbled yourself
before the Lord . . .
I also have heard you."

2 KINGS 22:19 NKJV

No Laughing Matter

J essica was concerned about her teenage son, Brad. He made a joke out of everything. Sometimes he was funny, but most of the time he was just obnoxious. During class, he spent more time goofing off than listening or contributing. And at church—when she could get him to church—he found something hilarious in the music, the pastor, and even the prayers. Even his friends refused to see the humor in his comments.

But that changed one Thursday night. That's when his father suffered a heart attack. At first, he'd tried to laugh it off, but after visiting his frail father in the hospital, there wasn't any humor left in Brad. Jessica had been praying for him and his father, and with this complication, she saw an immediate change.

The following Sunday at church, Brad didn't make fun of the music, the pastor, or even the prayers. Instead, he listened and allowed God to turn his empty laughter into inner joy—an experience that he told his father about later that day.

Jessica knew that humor is a wonderful thing, but Brad sometimes used it as a ploy to avoid making serious choices.

Do you use humor in the way God intended?

When you take life seriously, laughter tastes sweeter.

Your word is a lamp to my feet
and a light for my path.

PSALM 119:105

Your ears shall hear a word behind you,
saying, "This is the way, walk in it," when you
turn to the right or when you turn to the left.

ISAIAH 30:21 RSV

You will not leave in a hurry, running
for your lives. For the Lord will go
ahead of you, and the God of Israel
will protect you from behind.

ISAIAH 52:12 NLT

*Life is a road map that
God unfolds a day at a time.*

Winning Strategy

Pin the tail on the donkey wasn't just her children's party game. Jennie felt like it was her life. She didn't need a blindfold or a few disorienting twirls from a friend. Life was already confusing enough. In both cases you pray you don't trip over anything in your path. The only things guiding you are your gut instinct and the disheartening laughter of everyone as you head the wrong way. Only for her it seemed as if the blindfold never came off.

Then one day she read a chapter in her Bible, praying, "Please help me understand things." Things made sense that day. So she read and prayed the next day and the next. Jennie felt a new sense of peace, and what she still didn't understand she knew she could leave in God's hands. She could see Him when she couldn't see anything else.

God doesn't leave you blindfolded as you stumble through life. He's given you the Bible. It has a key that will help you understand how to read it. God's key is prayer. Try it!

I have kept the ways of the Lord;
I have not turned from
my God to follow evil.

PSALM 18:21 NLT

The integrity of the upright guides them,
but the crookedness of the
treacherous destroys them.

PROVERBS 11:3 RSV

By standing firm you will gain life.

LUKE 21:19

Everywhere

Considering how long it took to get her promotion, it was quite a shock for Penny's friends and extended family when they heard she'd quit her job. In disbelief they said, "You're kidding, right?" "What are you doing?" and "I can't believe it!"

What her children and husband, Dan, knew that others didn't know was how good Penny felt to leave a company that prided itself on deception. All her friends could see was the glory and prestige of a vice president's title—and the huge paycheck. But Penny and Dan saw how the almighty dollar had turned good people into power-hungry rule-benders. No matter how good the money was, they recognized that it was time for Penny to move on. And Penny knew her kids were watching her and learning more than the latest family news.

Living a life of integrity can mean big sacrifices at times. But those are the times when you have to do the right thing and trust God with the consequences. Remember, your children will learn more from what you do than what you say.

Our heavenly Father never takes anything from his children unless he means to give them something better.

Create in me a pure heart, O God.

PSALM 51:10

The comforter, which is the
Holy Ghost, whom the Father
will send in my name, he shall
teach you all things, and bring
all things to your remembrance,
whatsoever I have said unto you.

JOHN 14:26 KJV

You will restore me to even greater
honor and comfort me once again.

PSALM 71:21 NLT

Recipe for Righteousness

Chubby fingers clumsily cracked the egg on the side of the bowl. "Good, Garrett! Much better than last time," said Patrice, fishing out a stray eggshell. "Why don't you put in the sugar?"

As Patrice turned toward the pantry to get the oil, Garrett grabbed the yellow box, emptying it into the bowl. When Patrice returned, she noticed the cup of sugar was still full. The empty box of baking soda lay on its side, confirming her suspicions. "Well, Garrett," she sighed, "we're going to have to start over." She dumped the concoction in the sink as Garrett began to cry. "It's okay, honey; it's just a mistake," she soothed.

Wouldn't it be great if we never made mistakes? But we all do—big ones and small ones. Only the miracle of God's love and forgiveness can take our bumbling attempts and make them worthwhile.

What surrounds your life will eventually work its way inside.

Trust in the Lord and do good.

PSALM 37:3

Great peace have they which love thy law:
and nothing shall offend them.

PSALM 119:165 KJV

Therefore, since we are justified
by faith, we have peace with God
through our Lord Jesus Christ.

ROMANS 5:1 RSV

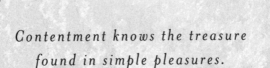

*Contentment knows the treasure
found in simple pleasures.*

Elementary Essentials

Deana stood behind the swings and listened to her children laughing as her husband sent them soaring. She hadn't had this much fun in a long time. Somehow eating out and seeing the latest techno-thriller had erased just how much fun it could be just to play. Life's joys were simpler than she'd realized lately.

Maybe I should simplify other things, she thought. Her time with God came to mind. All the colored pencils and workbooks had somehow chased God away. She was so busy "doing" Bible study that she barely noticed Him.

She felt God drawing near with that thought. "Maybe we could sit and just talk, God," she prayed. That sounded really wonderful somehow. She couldn't wait!

There's a lot about God's character and the Bible that isn't easily understood. But we can lose sight of the simple pleasure of God's presence. Spend some time just chatting with God.

"Look at the birds, free and unfettered,
not tied down to a job description,
careless in the care of God. And you
count far more to him than the birds."

MATTHEW 6:26 THE MESSAGE

But God's mercy is great, and he loved us
very much. Though we were spiritually
dead because of the things we did against
God, he gave us new life with Christ.
You have been saved by God's grace.

EPHESIANS 2:4-5 NCV

We know how much God loves us,
and we have put our trust in him.
God is love, and all who live in love
live in God, and God lives in them.

1 JOHN 4:16 NLT

More Than a Whole Lot

"How much does God love me?" Wesley asked his mother.

"More than He loves the birds and the butterflies," she replied.

"Does He love me more than race cars?"

"Yes, honey."

"More than getting a home run in a baseball game?"

"Yes."

"Wow!"

Wesley went back to the business of digging in the dirt. His little plastic shovel scooped up the sandy soil and poured it into the yellow dump truck. Just then a tiny bird flew to the ground beyond his construction site. Wesley dared not move. A moment later, the bird flew off with a wriggling worm in its beak.

"Mom," whispered Wesley. "Did you see that? That bird got some lunch. That was the coolest thing. Mom," he said as he rolled his truck toward the garden. "If God loves me more than birds, He must love me more than a whole lot, don't you think?"

God loves you as well— more than a whole lot!

God's love is bigger than your mind can grasp, but shared in bite-sized pieces you can taste.

When life gets really difficult,
don't jump to the conclusion
that God isn't on the job.

1 PETER 4:12 THE MESSAGE

"Remember, your Father knows
exactly what you need even
before you ask him!"

MATTHEW 6:8 TLB

Hope does not disappoint us,
because God has poured out his love
into our hearts by the Holy Spirit,
whom he has given us.

ROMANS 5:5

Disappearing Act?

Jessica's world looked a lot like the inside of the computer she had torn apart at home. Wires went every which way, complex circuits hung loosely from their moorings, and a shoddy power supply threatened to blow the whole thing up without so much as a warning buzzer.

The challenges of a difficult job, pressures of being a single mom, and pain caused by her father's recent illness all contributed to Jessica's stress. When the problems seemed particularly impossible, she would cry out, "Where are You, God?" And, for a while, she'd be certain God had disappeared. In time, though, Jessica would rediscover God's closeness and wonder if perhaps she had been the one who had left.

Every time she was sure God had gone on vacation, she would read the Bible and remember that God's ways are different from our ways. A solution was coming, but it might not look anything like what she was expecting.

God's answers don't often resemble our own.

If you don't see God in the middle of your trials, maybe you're looking in the wrong direction.

Like a weaned child with its mother,
like a weaned child is my soul within me.

PSALM 131:2

"My sheep hear my voice, and I know them, and
they follow me: and I give unto them eternal
life; and they shall never perish, neither
shall any man pluck them out of my hand."

JOHN 10:27-28 KJV

In Him you also trusted, after you heard
the word of truth, the gospel of your salvation;
in whom also, having believed, you were
sealed with the Holy Spirit of promise,
who is the guarantee of our inheritance
until the redemption of the purchased
possession, to the praise of His glory.

EPHESIANS 1:13-14 NKJV

*Peace isn't determined by what's
going on around you, as much as
by what's going on inside you.*

Quiet Time

Lauren rocked and looked at her toddler's chubby cheeks resting against her chest. She looked at her baby's arms completely still, the rhythmic breathing of her undisturbed slumber. She thought, *What more peaceful picture is there than this? Andrea is totally relaxed and trusts me enough to sleep in my lap. She is so secure in my love.*

Have you grown to trust God enough to relax in His arms? Your relationship with Him may seem comfortable when life is going your way, but how about when you're facing a crisis, when you're hurting, or when you're angry? What about the times when you can't seem to hear His voice?

God is a Parent whose love never fails. He wants you to lean on Him. Take time to crawl into God's lap today. Then just relax and enjoy the One who will never let you down.

There's no such thing as self-rescue,
pulling yourself up by your bootstraps.

PSALM 49:7 THE MESSAGE

Two people can accomplish more than
twice as much as one; they get a better return
for their labor. If one person falls, the other
can reach out and help. But people who are
alone when they fall are in real trouble.

ECCLESIASTES 4:9-10 NLT

By helping each other with your troubles,
you truly obey the law of Christ.

GALATIANS 6:2 NCV

On Your Own

As the youth group she led looked on, Hope reached for the next rung of the rope ladder. Little by little, she inched her way to the top of the wall and slid over. As she reached over to the swinging rope, her right foot caught in a looped rope. Suddenly, she was hanging upside down, fifteen feet off the ground. She knew that the safety harness would hold her, but she dangled in a humiliating position.

Straining every muscle, she tried to right herself, but no matter how hard she tried, she couldn't do it alone. "I'm on my way, Mom," she heard her son call. Derrick, of all people, had started climbing up after her. What would the kids think now?

In that moment as she waited for Derrick, Hope realized God was teaching her something. It was not only difficult for her to ask for help, it was almost impossible. "I get the message, Lord," Hope said, with a sigh. She would remember this lesson.

Sometimes the only way to save yourself is to ask someone else for help.

"I've come to change everything,
turn everything right side up."

LUKE 12:50 THE MESSAGE

"This is my command:
Love each other as I have loved you."

JOHN 15:12 NCV

"Then the King will say to those on
His right hand, 'Come, you blessed of
My Father, inherit the kingdom prepared
for you from the foundation of the world:
for I was hungry and you gave Me food;
I was thirsty and you gave Me drink;
I was a stranger and you took Me in.'"

MATTHEW 25:34-35 NKJV

A Little Out of the Way

On the stretch of highway where Kate's old clunker had broken down, hundreds of cars passed by without a second glance. That is, until one person stopped.

Cynthia pulled over a quarter mile beyond the stalled car and backed up slowly. "My kids and I are heading for a soccer tournament," she said, "but I have a few minutes. Can I help?"

Kate described the sudden, grinding halt, but Cynthia could offer no easy fix for her car. "I was heading to my sister's wedding," Kate said. "Could you please drive me to a phone?"

"I'd be glad to," Cynthia answered. "Let me help you with your stuff." Relieved, Kate grabbed her suitcases and climbed into the car. Then she wondered why a busy soccer mom, of all people, would be the one to give her a hand.

Helping others is almost never convenient, but it is always pleasing to God.

What you give to humanity you get back. Bread cast upon the waters is much more wholesome and nourishing than pie in the sky.

The Lord blesses his people with peace.

PSALM 29:11

Though wilt keep him in perfect
peace, whose mind is stayed on thee:
because he trusteth in thee.

ISAIAH 26:3 KJV

Embrace peace—don't let it get away!

PSALM 34:14 THE MESSAGE

*Peace isn't the absence of conflict;
it's knowing you're still loved
in the middle of it.*

Harried

Looking around the large room, you wouldn't think of it as a peaceful place. Toys, books, and small shoes occupied nearly every square inch of floor. Moments earlier, eight happy, noisy children had been jumping up and down, vying for their mom's attention.

But now the kids were outside, enjoying a perfect afternoon on the slides, swings, and teeter-totters. Nan carefully prepared the juice and graham crackers for an afternoon snack. She paused to think about her world. Though it was filled with tiny, loud, gap-toothed balls of energy, it was a peaceful world. Nan made it a safe place. *The kids may be loud,* Nan thought, *but my love for them is louder.* Then she realized, *God's love for me is loud too!*

God's love for you is louder than any other sound in your life. Are you dealing with some loud sounds today? Open your heart to listen, and you'll hear God calling to you through the din.

The man of integrity walks securely.

PROVERBS 10:9

I know, my God, that you test men to see
if they are good; for you enjoy good men.
I have done all this with good motives.

1 CHRONICLES 29:17 TLB

Til I die I will not put away
my integrity from me.

JOB 27:5 RSV

Confident Steps

"I have to do this, Tiffany," Melinda said. "I can't stay silent." Tiffany just shook her head and said, "This could mean your treasury seat on the PTA. Hey, it could mean my position too."

"We didn't do anything wrong," Melinda reminded her.

"I know," she said, "but the president did. What if he got his ideas from the vice president?"

"I don't have to mention your name," Melinda said.

Tiffany paused, then replied, "No, as much as I enjoy my position on the PTA, we have to confront this. I suppose if we do lose our positions, they can't keep us from volunteering in the classrooms." Melinda smiled at her friend, then gathered the file folders and marched into the copier room where the PTA vice president was working. She could feel God's approval, and it made her strong.

Melinda had carefully weighed her decision to blow the whistle on corruption. Being a person of integrity has its risks, but it is always the right thing to do.

Do you have the courage to do the right thing regardless of the consequences? Do your kids know that about you?

A person of integrity is someone who believes and lives the truth whether in the middle of a thunderstorm or thunderous applause.

Those who plan what is good
find love and faithfulness.

PROVERBS 14:22

Work with enthusiasm, as though
you were working for the Lord rather
than for people. Remember that the
Lord will reward each one of us for the
good we do, whether we are slaves or free.

EPHESIANS 6:7-8 NLT

Depart from evil, and do good;
and dwell forevermore.

PSALM 37:27 NKJV

Intentions

Caitlin looked puzzled. She was certain she'd set enough chairs around the table, but now she was holding an extra plate. Did she miscount the chairs or the plates? "Scott, how many plates did you give to me?"

"Sixteen."

"Mom, you missed one on the piano bench," said her son Kyle as he laid out silverware.

"Jerry's going to be here with a van full of people any minute," Scott said. "Could you make some coffee?" Nervous, she walked into the kitchen. "This is going to be an adventure, isn't it?" Scott said as she turned and smiled at him.

"I'll say," Kyle piped in from the dining room.

Caitlin hadn't been so certain until she talked with Hattie, one of their invited guests. She'd been at the homeless shelter for a month. "You don't know how much this means to me," she'd said tearfully. "This is going to be the best Thanksgiving ever." As Caitlin smiled back at Hattie, Scott agreed.

Make certain your plans are good: soak them overnight in selflessness.

A just man falleth seven times,
and riseth up again.

PROVERBS 24:16 KJV

The Lord upholds all who are falling,
and raises up all who are bowed down.

PSALM 145:14 RSV

When you're in over your head, I'll be
there with you. When you're in rough waters,
you will not go down. When you're between a
rock and a hard place, it won't be a dead end—
because I am God, your personal God,
the Holy of Israel, your Savior.

ISAIAH 43:2-3 THE MESSAGE

*The drop of rain maketh a hole
in the stone, not by violence,
but by oft falling.*

Not Down for the Count

"**D**id you see that?" Larry asked as he sat transfixed by the actions of his two-year-old. "Look, he's trying again." His son, Alex, stretched out his stubby fingers, reaching for the shiny plastic object just out of reach. "That's six times he's tried to reach that plate, and six times he's landed on his rear end."

"Honey, why don't you reach it for him?" Rhonda suggested, even though they both knew it was more important for Alex to succeed alone. One more try—yes!

"Way to go, son!" Larry said to a beaming Alex. Rhonda watched and wondered how many more times Alex would fall in his life. Why did the path to adulthood have to be so littered with obstacles? As she walked over to help him stand, she prayed silently, *Dear Lord, I know Alex is going to fall as he grows up. Please always be there to help him up.*

We all fall down a lot in life, but God is always there to help us up.

The path of the righteous is like
the light of dawn, which shines
brighter and brighter until full day.

PROVERBS 4:18 RSV

Seek his will in all you do,
and He will direct your paths.

PROVERBS 3:6 NLT

You are my rock and my protection.
For the good of your name,
lead me and guide me.

PSALM 31:3 NCV

Give God a Turn

Jill sat at the coffee table with her Bible and cup of coffee. She felt as though she had endured an entire day, and it was only 8:40 A.M. Mornings with her 14-year-old son seemed to suck every ounce of strength from her. Thomas had been such an easy child until last year. Now it felt like every conversation became a confrontation, and Jill was tired of standing her ground.

"God, I want to give up and let him do his own thing," Jill cried aloud. "He's so strong-willed and determined to do things opposite of my wishes. Why won't he listen? I can save him so much heartache if he'll listen," Jill prayed. "I can't do this anymore."

I can save you from heartache, she felt God say to her, *Give me a turn.* Immediately a new strength filled Jill's heart. A glimpse of God's heart for her success as a mother provided a new strength.

Jill realized it was time to let go. God knew and loved Thomas as much—more—than she did. "Okay, God, it's Your turn. I'm letting go."

That afternoon Thomas came home with a song on his lips. His humming caused Jill to silently thank God again. She could already see a change in her son's countenance and in her own heart.

> *The weaker we feel, the harder we lean on God. And the harder we lean, the stronger we grow.*

If you let go, God will take His turn—and turn it around.

Do not be anxious about anything,
but in everything, by prayer
and petition, with thanksgiving,
present your requests to God.

PHILIPPIANS 4:6

I have trusted the Lord
and never doubted.

PSALM 26:1 NCV

Give all your worries and cares to God,
for he cares about what happens to you.

1 PETER 5:7 NLT

Reserved Parking

Dana was on the last leg of her mission. She'd been to the bank, post office, and now, if she could buzz through the grocery store for the few things she needed before the twins passed out in their car seats for their after-noon nap, it would be smooth sailing.

Her hopes dashed as she turned into the parking lot. It looked as though every spot was filled. "God, I feel silly asking this," Dana prayed, "but I need Your peace—and a parking spot I can get into!" A truck abruptly pulled out in front of her car. After slamming on her brakes, she noticed the driver had just vacated an oversized spot directly across from the entry doors and next to an empty cart she could easily put the twins into. Dana took a moment to breathe and to offer thanks.

Prayer isn't reserved for life-and-death situations. If you're anxious, talk to God. He won't always change your circumstances, but His peace and presence will certainly change your focus.

Whate'er we leave to God, God does. And blesses us.

It is better to take refuge in the
Lord than to trust in man.

PSALM 118:8

There are many plans in a
man's heart, nevertheless the
Lord's counsel—that will stand.

PROVERBS 19:21 NKJV

The Lord, your Redeemer, the Holy One
of Israel, says: "I am the Lord your God,
who teaches you what is good and leads you
along the paths you should follow."

ISAIAH 48:17 NLT

Men give advice;
God gives guidance.

Mixed Signals

Meg felt like she was getting conflicting advice from the Scarecrow in the "Wizard of Oz." *What should she do?* she wondered. Tina said, "Leave him." Grace said, "You need to confront him." And Hallie said, "Tell him if he doesn't get some help, you're out of there."

Alan wasn't a bad person. Since their wedding, they'd enjoyed an idyllic life. He didn't start drinking until she miscarried their second child. Meg knew he had taken it hard. She also knew the warning signs of alcoholism, having watched her father take that path. None of her friends' advice sounded quite right. Instead, Meg prayed, and she searched the Bible for insight.

When she finally approached Alan, she did so with love and concern. She didn't blow up, she didn't make threats, and she didn't condemn. She talked and listened. Within a week, he had begun a twelve-step program—and she had taken twelve steps closer to God.

Make the most of every opportunity.

COLOSSIANS 4:5

Kind words are like honey—sweet to
the soul and healthy for the body.

PROVERBS 16:24 NLT

A word fitly spoken is like apples
of gold in a setting of silver.

PROVERBS 25:11 RSV

Five Minutes

"I've got five minutes, Nikki. What's so important?" Mandy demanded.

Nikki nervously shifted her weight back and forth. How was she going to say this? "Mandy, there's something I've been meaning to tell you."

Her friend's smile quickly faded, and she asked, "What? Is something wrong?"

Nikki shook her head and replied, "No, it's just that, well, you and I have been friends a long time, right?"

"Right."

"And you know I'm one of those church-going people."

"Yes . . ."

"The thing is, I've never told you what makes my life so complete."

Mandy glanced at her watch. "Three minutes," she said.

"Mandy, remember how you've said, 'There's something different about you'?"

"Yes—two minutes."

"Well, that something is my relationship with God. I shouldn't have waited so long to tell you this, but you'll be gone for so long, and I want you to know what I know."

"Thanks," Mandy said with a smile.

Those around you need God in their lives. Don't put off sharing your faith.

An ounce of testimony is worth a ton of propaganda.

"With God all things are possible."

MATTHEW 19:26

Such is the confidence that we have
through Christ toward God. Not that
we are competent of ourselves to claim
anything as coming from us;
our competence is from God.

2 CORINTHIANS 3:4-5 RSV

Behold, the Lord thy God hath set the land
before thee: go up and possess it, as the Lord
God of thy fathers hath said unto thee;
fear not, neither be discouraged.

DEUTERONOMY 1:21 KJV

Beyond the Impossible

As they drove up the hill, Lori's heart was racing. "I don't know if I can do this, Sam," she said in desperation. "I love my own children, but I don't know these children." In the valley below, dozens of children would be waiting. Sam said they always knew when to congregate, even though none wore a watch. Somehow, everyone knew when the truck—packed with food, tools, and supplies—was on its way down the mountain.

Lori protested when she'd been picked to help. "How can I communicate if I don't know their language?" Sam simply smiled and reassured her everything would be fine. The truck skidded to a stop in a cloud of dust.

Immediately, a crowd of dirty, smiling faces swarmed around her. "I can do this," she said as one smiling little boy came up and gave her a giant hug. She then looked heavenward, and said, "You can do this through me, God."

The one who can see the invisible can do the impossible.

When God gives us an assignment, He's always there to help us carry it out.

Am I now trying to win the
approval of men, or of God?

GALATIANS 1:10

Where jealousy and selfish
ambition exist, there will be
disorder and every vile practice.

JAMES 3:16 RSV

Then I observed that the basic motive
for success is the driving force
of envy and jealousy! But this, too,
is foolishness, chasing the wind.

ECCLESIASTES 4:4 TLB

*The only reputation
that matters is your
reputation in Heaven.*

Impressive

"This is one of the largest structures of its kind. Indeed, it is a tribute to one man's ingenuity and persever- ance." The disembodied voice trailed off as Molly stared at the building. It towered over the surrounding structures, which—in any other city—would have loomed large.

Why do people build these huge buildings? she thought. *Certainly it's not for all the office space. There are plenty of empty buildings in this city.* She unexpectedly got her answer from her five-year-old son sitting next to her on the tour bus.

"Mom, when I grow up, I want to build an even bigger building so they'll drive around and talk about me on the tour!" Of course! Ultimately, it was about someone wanting to look good.

Whose approval do you work for? Sometimes mothering can be a lonely job with little respect. But in God's eyes children are much more important than large buildings.

You know that under pressure,
your faith-life is forced into the open
and shows its true colors.

JAMES 1:3 THE MESSAGE

Do not be ashamed to testify about our Lord,
or ashamed of me his prisoner.

2 TIMOTHY 1:8

We do not distort the word of God.
We tell the truth before God,
and all who are honest know that.

2 CORINTHIANS 4:2 NLT

Inside Out

This would be Bridget's biggest test. Sitting around a game table with a bunch of friends from work had been a Saturday tradition for weeks. But on this night, the taboo subject of religion had been broached.

"I think all religions are crutches," Marty said.

"I used to go to church," added Kate, "but all I got out of it was guilt and depression." Bridget waited for Amelia to say something, but she remained silent. "What about you, Bridget? What do you think?" Kate asked.

Before Bridget could answer, her sixteen-year-old daughter, Brooke, eavesdropping at the kitchen sink, piped up, "I think it takes guts to have faith in a God you can't see."

"How so?" Marty replied, looking at Bridget, readying his attack.

"Take sitting around this table and admitting you're a Christian," Amelia commented. "Doesn't that take guts?" Marty shrugged. "Then observe gutsy: I'm a Christian."

A rather surprised Bridget added, "So am I." It was the beginning of the most invigorating game-night discussion they'd ever had.

How gutsy are you about your faith? Do your friends know you are a believer?

> *Where one man reads the Bible, a hundred read you and me.*

He heals the heartbroken
and bandages their wounds.

PSALM 147:3 THE MESSAGE

Yes, I will bless the Lord and not forget
the glorious things he does for me.
He forgives all my sins. He heals me.

PSALM 103:2-3 TLB

He comforts us every time we
have trouble, so when others have
trouble, we can comfort them with
the same comfort God gives us.

2 CORINTHIANS 1:4 NCV

We Need a Bigger Bandage

In all of Sue's years as a nurse, she had never seen a wound as deep as this one. Her son Michael's fiancée had called off the wedding. He sat before Sue with his head in his hands, crying inconsolably. He asked, "Why did this happen to me?"

Sue grabbed a roll of gauze and set it on the table. "Michael, I can bandage dozens of injuries with this gauze, but I don't think it can heal a broken heart." He looked up at his mother without smiling. "I can't make the pain go away," Sue continued, "but I can pray for you."

"Then pray for me," he said.

"Dear Lord," Sue prayed, "Michael is hurting—big time. You know what it's like to be brokenhearted. Be with him in this tough time."

When Sue finished, Michael looked up with a puzzled expression and asked, "What does God know about being brokenhearted?" At that moment, Nancy knew God was also going to use her to heal the pain of her son's empty heart.

Is someone in your family hurting? Let them see you praying for them.

God's bandages work wonders on hurting hearts.

God doesn't want us to be shy with his gifts,
but bold and loving and sensible.

2 TIMOTHY 1:7 THE MESSAGE

Whatever your hand finds to do,
do it with your might.

ECCLESIASTES 9:10 RSV

Do you see a man who excels at his work?
He will stand before kings;
he will not stand before unknown men.

PROVERBS 22:29 NKJV

*God's gifts may look like
fine china, but they're meant
to be used like everyday dishes.*

Waking Up to Singing

Jerry woke up to Helen's singing just about every Saturday morning. His wife enjoyed her weekday work—though teaching's rewards were often not realized until years after the children had graduated. But Saturday was the day for her family to feel the warmth and encouragement that flowed like a fountain from her.

Helen sang everything from hymns to rock and roll. It didn't matter, really. She was an encouraging person, and the sound of her joy-filled voice was enough to start the day off right. During the weekdays, her uplifting words fed the starving hearts and minds of teenagers. "Middle school students are the toughest to teach," she once said to a friend. "That's because they need more encouragement."

But it was Saturday, and Helen was singing again. Jerry thanked God for giving his wife the gift of encouragement. It was just what those students needed—and he needed it too.

Has God given you a gift that you could share with your family and others?

Never walk away from someone
who deserves help; your hand
is God's hand for that person.

PROVERBS 3:27 THE MESSAGE

When God's children are in need,
be the one to help them out.

ROMANS 12:13 NLT

In all things I have shown you
that by so toiling one must help
the weak, remembering the words
of the Lord Jesus, how he said,
"It is more blessed to give than to receive."

ACTS 20:35 RSV

Moment of Decision

The lost look on the teenage girl's face told much of the story. Edna sat with her on a long, hard bench at the bus station to hear the rest. "My parents divorced when I just was a kid," she began.

Edna listened to the whole story before asking, "What do you need?" She was certain the girl would ask for money or a bus ticket or something to help her get as far away as possible from her past.

"I—just want someone to care about me," she finally stammered. Edna hesitated. She could either walk away, or she could make an investment in the life of this heartsick teenager. Reaching out would cost a bundle in time, money, and hassles; but the cost of not doing so was too big to calculate. She could only imagine if this had been her own daughter. She would want someone to reach out to her. "God cares about you," she said, "and I want to help. Can we call your foster parents first? They must be worried sick about you."

A bit of fragrance always clings to the hand that gives you roses.

Celebrate God all day, every day,
I mean, revel in him!

PHILIPPIANS 4:4 THE MESSAGE

Go and celebrate. . . .
This is a sacred day before our Lord.
Don't be dejected and sad, for the
joy of the Lord is your strength!

NEHEMIAH 8:10 NLT

"You shall go out in joy, and be
led forth in peace; the mountains
and the hills before you shall break
forth into singing, and all the trees
of the field shall clap their hands."

ISAIAH 55:12 RSV

Wake Up Smiling

"Hey, honey! It's morning! It's an incredible, wonderful morning!" Nicole rolled over and looked up through blurry eyes at her giddy husband who was doing jumping jacks next to the bed.

"What time is it?" she groaned. "And what's the phone number for the loony bin?"

Ray laughed and jumped up onto the bed like it was a trampoline. "Life is good, Nicole. God is good! Everything is good!"

"What's up?" she asked.

"I just want to throw myself into life," he replied, "to celebrate God's goodness in a silly, over-the-top way. Come on, jump on the bed with me."

Nicole tried to fight the smile, but it was too late. He had already seen it. "Come on," he pleaded. Their three-year-old, Timmy, was quick to join the fun. Nicole clumsily climbed to her feet and held Ray's hands. Together, they jumped on the bed, laughing, falling, and thanking God at the top of their lungs.

When was the last time you shared the joy of life with someone?

Joy shared is joy doubled.

The lines of purpose in your lives
never grow slack, tightly tied as they are to
your future in heaven, kept taut by hope.

COLOSSIANS 1:5 THE MESSAGE

True humility and fear of the Lord
lead to riches, honor, and long life.

PROVERBS 22:4 NLT

When the righteous cry for help,
the Lord hears, and delivers
them out of all their troubles.

PSALM 34:17 RSV

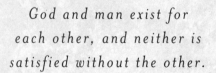

*God and man exist for
each other, and neither is
satisfied without the other.*

Trajectory

"Don't tell me about direction!" Lana shot back from her lounge chair. "I've been dancing all my life."

"But look where you are now, Sis. You *have* no direction."

Though Lana hated to admit it, Elise was right. One misstep during rehearsal and her dreams of being a dancer were over. "Well, I don't see you practicing medicine yet!" she countered.

Lana saw Elise looking at her intently. Lana knew the lines around her eyes were deeper than the last time that Elise had visited her in the hospital. "My life's purpose is bigger than my career, Lana. I may not be a doctor yet—or ever. But I know I'm where God wants me."

As always, Lana squirmed at the mention of God. He had never been part of her long-range plans. "Is that what keeps you going, Elise?"

"Yeah, God—and hope," she answered.

After a long silence, Lana asked in a small, tired voice. "Do you think God can help me?"

Do you forget to ask God for His help? He is always there for you.

"Life is not defined by what you have,
even when you have a lot."

LUKE 12:15 THE MESSAGE

Work instead at what is right and good,
learning to trust Him and love others,
and to be patient and gentle.

1 TIMOTHY 6:11 TLB

He will love thee, and bless thee,
and multiply thee.

DEUTERONOMY 7:13 KJV

Garage Sale

Natalie and Steven had accumulated lots of "stuff," thanks to both of their successful careers in sales. That stuff included three vehicles, a pool table, seven televisions, and more furniture than most small stores.

A few months ago Natalie would have said, "We have everything we could ever want since Thomas was born." Well, everything except a meaningful life. That changed when they followed Thomas to church when he was invited to go with a friend. They found what they'd been missing for so many years. Turns out, they'd been missing everything.

Now that their whole family has a thriving relationship with God, Nicole has revised her priorities. She's simplifying her life, and that means one thing—garage sale. "Too much stuff gets in the way of who God wants me to be," she told a possible buyer for the big-screen TV. Even though Nicole is retired, she's still in sales. Now she sells people an opportunity to meet God.

Once we've known the love of God, life takes on a whole new meaning.

All that we possess is qualified by what we are.

Your life is a journey you must travel
with a deep consciousness of God.

1 PETER 1:17 THE MESSAGE

"Behold, I am with you and will keep you
wherever you go, and will bring you back to
this land; for I will not leave you until I have
done that of which I have spoken to you."

GENESIS 28:15 RSV

If you make the Most High your
dwelling—even the LORD, who is my
refuge—then no harm will befall you,
no disaster will come near your tent.

PSALM 91:9-10

Traveling Companion

The thirty or more photo albums on Stacey's table protected only a small percentage of the photographs she'd taken in the past four years. The rest of the pictures filled four large blue bins now stored under the dining room table.

The brown albums chronicled Stacey's three months in Asia. The blue albums were filled with pictures from Europe. Black albums featured memories from her year in Australia, and tan albums showcased images from Africa and South America.

In her four years of continent hopping, she had learned more about the world and its people than a lifetime of schooling could ever have taught her. She'd flown over Victoria Falls, climbed the Eiffel Tower, dodged crazy drivers in downtown Tokyo, and shared a meal with members of the ancient Maori tribe. But the most valuable lesson she had learned was something she had known as she walked to school in Louisiana twenty years earlier and now shared with her son as he packed his truck for college: God makes a great travel companion.

When you go on vacation, take God with you.

When you leave home, pack your Bible and plan to spend time with the One who made the world you travel.

I can always count on you—
God, my dependable love.

PSALM 59:17 THE MESSAGE

The Lord your God will make you most
prosperous in all the work of your hands.

DEUTERONOMY 30:9

He shall be like a tree planted by the
rivers of water, that brings forth its fruit in
its season, whose leaf also shall not wither;
and whatever he does shall prosper.

PSALM 1:3 NKJV

*The reward of a good deed
is to have done it.*

No-Shows

"There were supposed to be eleven more people to help out," Bev complained, sweeping a corner of the warehouse that had been cleared of boxes. "Something must have come up."

"For all eleven at the same time?" Irene said, sliding a box into the truck. "I don't think so. They were no-shows."

"Oh, well, so what if it's just the five of us," Bev said, trying to put a positive spin on things as she looked at her toddler playing in the dirt with Irene's two boys. "We're probably the best cleaners in the group anyway."

Irene laughed and said, "Now there's something to put on my résumé."

"Irene," Ben chided, pouring a dustpan full of dirt into the trash barrel.

"You're right, Bev. I guess I should be more positive," she said as she stacked another box. "Hard to believe this is going to be a soup kitchen."

Bev surveyed the big room and said, "The project director did say that we were a Godsend. Look how much we did today, Irene. Maybe we had some help today after all."

God keeps his word even when the
whole world is lying through its teeth.

ROMANS 3:4 THE MESSAGE

Yes, dear friends, we are already God's
children, and we can't even imagine what we
will be like when Christ returns. But we do
know that when he comes we will be like him,
for we will see him as he really is.

1 JOHN 3:2 NLT

For the Lord will not forsake His people;
He will not abandon His heritage;
for justice will return to the righteous,
and all the upright in heart will follow it.

PSALM 94:14-15 RSV

No More Promises

"**Y**ou said you'd be here for me." Tamara wasn't talking to anyone in particular. Or perhaps she was talking to everyone. But no one could hear her. She sat alone in the basement of a condemned apartment building, clutching a small bag that held everything she owned or had stolen, including a small Bible.

"You said you loved me." Promises made; promises broken. Those words defined Tamara's life. Parents promised love and gave none. Those she loved promised to be there and weren't. Friends promised a helping hand and did nothing. Even her children had abandoned her.

"Isn't there anyone left who tells the truth?" she yelled as she threw her bag against the graffiti-covered wall. The Bible landed a few feet in front of her. She glanced at it and wondered if God kept His promises. Slowly, she crawled over and picked up the Bible. "Don't lie to me, God. I couldn't take it," she pleaded. As she opened the Bible, she opened her heart just one more time. And she felt that this time it would be different.

God's promises are like the stars; the darker the night, the brighter they shine.

Do you sometimes feel that no one cares, that no one keeps his word? God is always there for you. Seek Him and find out just how much He cares.

When they had finished eating, Jesus said
to Simon Peter, "Simon son of John,
do you truly love me more than these?"

JOHN 21:15

Why is everyone hungry for more? "More,
more," they say. "More, more."
I have God's more-than-enough,
more joy in one ordinary day
than they get in all their shopping sprees.
At day's end I'm ready for sound sleep,
for you, God, have put my life back together.

PSALM 4:6-8 THE MESSAGE

"Keep company with me and you'll
learn to live freely and lightly."

MATTHEW 11:30 THE MESSAGE

More Than These?

Patricia sat on the porch stoop watching Brian toddle over to the sandbox full of cars and trucks. Celia was asleep in her stroller behind her in the kitchen. It was a quiet moment. She sighed. Something inside wasn't happy, and she didn't know where it came from. She loved her children, her home, and her goofy, loving husband. She had everything she had wanted all her life. What was wrong?

Inside she felt the answer rising to the surface: "Do you love Me more than these?"

"No," she said, tentatively. "I don't know, on second thought. I'm not happy, Lord. I don't know why. And I don't know if I love You." It all came spilling out with some tears and a tight feeling deep in her chest that began to ease as the flood of words sputtered to a stop. She could feel God was there and that her honesty had cleared things between them. She wanted to feel forever what she was feeling at that moment. She would try to be honest with Him more often.

For the one who confesses, shams are over and realities have begun.

How about you? Are the blessings of God keeping you from the blessing of God himself? Take some time. Be honest. And follow His lead.

Hear, O LORD, and answer me,
for I am poor and needy.

PSALM 86:1

Be strong in the Lord and
the strength of His might.

EPHESIANS 6:10 NASB

Keep on praying.

1 THESSALONIANS 5:17 NLT

*Anything large enough for
a wish to light upon is large
enough to hang a prayer on.*

God's Help

"Okay, Mom. I'm ready," said Sharon.

Angela dried her hands, laid one hand on Sharon's shoulder, and prayed, "Father, please help Sharon with her test today. And also we ask that You would help her friend Mimi to get better and come back to school."

"Don't forget about Janie," Sharon whispered, her eyes closed tightly for prayer.

"And, Father, we ask that You would please comfort Janie. You know she is very worried about her sick brother. Please make him well."

"Thanks, Mom. Oh, there's the bus! Gotta go!" With a slam of the back door, she was gone.

But Angela knew Sharon would be all right. Since they had begun praying in the morning about homework, tests, friends—all kinds of things—Sharon no longer had tearful mornings and grumpy nights. Angela had learned a lesson—they needed God's assistance to make it through their day. *Even mine,* she thought, heading to her "prayer chair" for her morning time with Him. She still had lots more to say.

We all need God's help. Spend some time today telling Him what you need, and don't forget to thank Him for what He has already done.

Her children rise up and bless her.

PROVERBS 31:28 NASB

"Honor your father and your mother
so that you may live long."

EXODUS 20:12

Stories we heard from our fathers,
counsel we learned at our mother's knee.
We're not keeping this to ourselves,
we're passing it along to the next
generation—God's fame and fortune,
the marvelous things he has done.

PSALM 78:3-4 THE MESSAGE

Don't Ever Forget

Andrea set the rose in the vase and tied a white ribbon around it. She knew her mother was in heaven, but on her birthday Andrea just felt a need to do something to remember her mother. One of the last things she had said to Andrea followed her everywhere—"Dear, what you do in the lives of these children will affect the world and eternity. Don't ever forget how important motherhood is, even if the world does."

"Mom, can we have some juice?" Stephen asked as he banged open the back door bringing in three friends.

"Sure," she said. "Sit at the table and I'll get it for you."

"Wow!" said Bill, the little boy from down the street. "Y'ur mom is nice!"

Later Andrea sat on the porch and watched them play. The sun shone; the street was quiet. She could hear the bees buzzing in the flowerbed. "O God, thank You for this moment. Thank You for all the things my mother taught me."

Everything you do as a mother is so very important to everyone your child will ever meet. Don't ever forget.

The mother's heart is the child's schoolroom.

Acknowledgements

Martha Washington (10), A. W. Tozer (13, 190), Mark Hopkins (19), Sir James M. Barrie (21), Soren Aabye Kierkegaard (22), W. S. Bowden (27), Dolores E. McGuire (28), William Shakespeare (31), Evelyn Underhill (33), Saint Augustine of Hippo (34), C. G. Jung (37), Jewish Proverb (39), John Miller (40), Oswald Chambers (43), Sir Winston Churchill (46), Charles Kingsley (55), Richard Owen Roberts (58), Billy Sunday (61), Meister Eckhart (63), George MacDonald (64), Thomas A Kempis (67), Irish Proverb (69), Irish Proverb (69), Jean Jacques Rousseau (70), William Penn (73), Hildebert of Lavardin (76), French Proverb (79), Edwin W. Lutzer (85), Saint Irenaeus (87), Roberta S. Curry (99), Jean-Paul Sartre (111), Ralph Waldo Emerson (112), Thomas Mann (123), Henry Ward Beecher (124), Dwight L. Moody (135, 181), Saint John of Damascus (136), George Mueller (145), Melvin Jones (159), Henry David Thoreau (171), Leonard Ravenhill (172), John Lancaster Spalding (193), Elbert Hubbard (196), David Nicholas (199).

Additional copies of this book and other titles in the
Glimpses of an Invisible God series are
available from your local bookstore.
Also look for our special gift editions in this series.

Glimpses of an Invisible God
Glimpses of an Invisible God for Teachers
Glimpses of an Invisible God for Teens
Glimpses of an Invisible God for Women

If you have enjoyed this book,
or if it has impacted your life,
we would like to hear from you.
Please contact us at:
Honor Books
An Imprint of Cook Communications Ministries
4050 Lee Vance View
Colorado Springs, CO 80918

Or by e-mail: www.cookministries.com